W9-AZJ-503

BICYCLING

TOURING AND MOUNTAIN BIKE BASICS

BY
PETER OLIVER

Introduction

by

John Viehman

A TRAILSIDE SERIES GUIDE

W.W. NORTON & COMPANY

NEW YORK LONDON

Printed in the United States of America

First Edition

The text of this book is composed in Bodoni Book with the display set in Triplex
Page composition by LaserImage
Color separations and prepress by Bergman Graphics, Incorporated
Manufacturing by R. R. Donnelley & Sons
Illustrations by Ron Hildebrand

Book design by Bill Harvey

Library of Congress Cataloging-in-Publication Data

Oliver, Peter, 1953—
Bicycling : touring & mountian bike basics / by Peter Oliver ;
introduction by John Viehman.
p. cm. — (A Trailside series guide)
A companion volume to the television series, Trailside.
Includes bibliographical references and index.
1. Cycling. I. Title. II. Series.
GV1041.054 1995 796.6:—dc20 95-5528

ISBN 0-393-31337-9

W. W. Norton & Company, Inc., 500 Fifth Avenue, New York, N. Y. 10110
W. W. Norton & Company Ltd., 10 Coptic Street, London WC1A 1PU

1 2 3 4 5 6 7 8 9 0

CONTENTS

INTRODUCTION

"Dad, none of the other kids are using training wheels...."

If a young daughter wants to get her dad's immediate and undivided attention, she only needs to hint that she's a little embarrassed to still be using training wheels. It ranks right up there with the first day of grade school and losing that first tooth. Some things strike a deep vein of proprietorship in the dad species, and bicycles are one of them.

I clearly remember the day I learned to ride a two-wheeler. I even remember the name of the friend who lent me her bike. I'd been on training wheels for ages, when one day I decided enough was enough. I hopped on the borrowed bike and started pedaling like mad. To realize that I could sail down the sidewalk sans training wheels was exhilarating, and easily the highlight of my short life. In a few yards, I had graduated from babyhood and rolled triumphantly into kidhood.

When my daughter was facing the same rite of passage, I was on the case. I dutifully asked other dads for advice, then adjusted it to accommodate my daughter's independent nature. (That's a polite way of saying she'd fight me tooth and nail if I didn't let her learn at her own pace.) I quickly realized there was no way that my daughter was going to learn to ride a bicycle the way I had, nor was she about to listen to my sermonizing on how to do it. This called for a different approach, so like legions of dads before me, I put on my running shoes and headed to the sidewalk with her. We spent hours and hours together with me running alongside, one hand firmly grasping her bike seat, while she tentatively zigzagged along.

First she learned not to lean too heavily on dad's arm, then she realized the value of keeping the pedals moving, then she started taking the wiggle out of the handlebars, and so it went. Miles of running for me; pedaling for her.

I watched as she slowly but surely coordinated the physical movements. Closer and closer she came to synchronizing everything. I ran some more; she pedaled. Days came and went. She wasn't going to quit, and she wasn't going to let me let her quit. After a couple weeks, the moment came when she pedaled beyond the movements and started focusing on the objective—where she wanted to go with the bike. That's when I knew I could let go of her bike seat. I lied at this stage, of course, and told her I was still holding on. She knew I was letting go, and sort of wanted me to anyway, so she let me get away with the illusion. I ran more miles and my arm relaxed; she pedaled as though nothing was different, but something certainly was.

When the bittersweet moment finally arrived, I stopped running and just stood there watching in awe and delight tinged with sadness as my daughter pedaled her way out of babyhood. She'd still need her dad in the years to come (or so I comforted myself), but she was on her own bike from now on—stiff-legs, flat feet, and all.

I've recalled this personal moment because I think it tells the story of this book. Like a good parent, author Peter Oliver has packed it full of time-proven advice, while taking great pains to stay out of the pulpit. His handiwork is ready to hold your bike seat through the most trying moments, then propel you beyond the pages and onto a new level of bicycling. Just like my daughter, though, he presupposes that you'll want to decide where and when to take that leap. Rest assured, he won't push you into becoming the super-athlete you never wanted to be or some sort of aerobic machine-on-wheels. No, this is bicycling on a human scale and reminds us all of the reason we enjoy bikes in the first place.

Before reading this book, I thought I knew everything I needed to know about riding a bike. Within a few pages, however, I realized how much I had forgotten, how much I'd never learned, and how much the world of bicycles had changed. Technology has made bicycles as simple or as complex as the individual rider's needs. The basic two-wheeler has evolved from mere toy to exercise station and transportation vehicle, on into racing machine, even art. Certainly it's enough to overwhelm any dad. Yet when I came to the last page I'd learned that there's a lot more to riding than just hopping on a borrowed bike. Better still, I was bursting with enthusiasm to ride. The kid in me had been revived.

I couldn't wait to feel the air whistling by me, the exhilaration of flying on wheels, the gentle, arcing sweep of a wide turn. Most of all, I couldn't wait to once again see the world transformed by the cyclist's perspective. It's nearly impossible to describe how different things look from the saddle. Although a lot of books have tried to capture it, few have succeeded. Mercifully, this one doesn't waste the space. Ultimately, bicycling remains something you must experience to fully appreciate. Once you do, watch out. There's no telling where your bicycle will take you.

So, welcome to kidhood!

—John Viehman

1
THE WHEEL THING

On a fine day in the fall of 1994, Miguel Indurain, the best bicycle racer in the world of the 90s, hopped on his bike and pedaled 53.040 kilometers—about 33 miles—in one hour. In doing so, the lanky Spaniard established a new record for the distance covered in an hour by a man on two wheels without the aid of a motor.

He received quite a lot of congratulatory acclaim for his feat, and deservedly so. Admirers slapped Miguel lustily on the back. They praised his mighty ride as a superhuman achievement, beyond the reach of mere mortal pedalers. It was a record, they reckoned, not soon to be broken.

But then wouldn't you know it—less than two months later, along comes Tony Rominger, the next-best racer in the world of the 1990s. Rominger saw a chance to stick it to his archrival by taking a shot at the one-hour record himself. Boarding his own sleek two-wheeler, Rominger briskly rang up 55.291 kilometers in an hour, thumping the superhuman stuffing right out of Indurain's short-lived reign as king of the one-hour ride. The cycling world gasped in collective disbelief, but then settled back to appreciate the wonderful mayhem that Rominger's 34.36-mph ride had wrought upon one of cycling's most cherished records. Faster than the immortal Indurain!

?

DID YOU KNOW

A Belgian newspaper, *Le Gaulois*, is credited with coining the term, "bicycle," in the 1890s. Before that—and in some places, thereafter—bikes were known primarily as velocipedes.

Who'd have thought it possible?

It is a rare moment when the average person exceeds 33 or 34 miles an hour on a bike, much less continues at that pace for a full hour. But neither the speed nor the endurance is the essential thing to be marveled at in the masterful riding of Rominger and Indurain. More to the point, their classic duel made a profound statement about bicycling's high place in that primal search for a bond between man and machine. Their back-to-back, record-breaking rides were a celebration of the seamless interface between a visceral, human effort and the metallic workings of a machine. Ergonomics, as it is called—the essence of riding a bike. To have watched Miguel Indurain or Tony Rominger chase the hour record would have been to witness man and bike working together as a finely tuned, synchronized, and inseparable synergistic unit.

The same would probably not be said of a kid set loose on the first, wobbly moments away from training wheels. The kid has things other than synergy to worry about—staying upright, for starters. Yet it's never long before she or he gets the basic hang of it. After only a few hours of teetering experimentation, the kid clicks in, summoning the ability and confidence to do essentially the same thing as the most accomplished racer: pump pedals and propel a bike forward.

In other words, riding a bike is not a complicated business. A kid can do it, not much differently if not necessarily as swiftly as the speedballing Rominger and Indurain. Riding a bike is only slightly more difficult, but considerably faster and more dynamic, than walking. A whole lot more fun, too. Not long after learning to stay upright, the kid becomes attuned to the rhythmic flow of the pedals, the sudden speed, the energy transfer from legs to pedals and finally to spinning wheels. It is one of the great, heady rushes of childhood, that discovery of the art of riding. And not long after that he or she is off doing wheelies, jumping curbs, sticking playing cards in the rear-wheel spokes, and showing off to friends an ability to ride without hands.

Now it is possible that there is someone of able body in the United States who doesn't know how to ride a bike, but such a person would be hard to find. Cycling is as common as

Riding through Rocky Mountain National Park: Two wheels, two pedals, and healthy lungs—the only things a person needs to strike out in exploration of the world's most beautiful places.

language, as familiar as buttoning a shirt. You never forget, as the saying goes. Of course, far too many people allow their unforgotten bike-riding ability to go woefully unpracticed. Nevertheless, cycling is ingrained enough in the American fabric that more bikes are sold in the United States in an average year than cars—11.6 million bikes in 1993, according to the Bicycle Federation of America. And that's peanuts compared with the countless millions of bikes infesting a place like China, a nation utterly dependent on the bicycle for its goings and comings.

No country in the world depends on bicycles as a means of transportation to the degree that China does.

That raises a point not to be missed: For all of its record-breaking potential at the highest level of sport, for all of the ways it is used recreationally, competitively, or as a child's plaything, the bike is, essentially, a means of transportation. It is a humble, utilitarian instrument. Where else in the recreational world do function, sport, and play come together in so neat a way? Baseball mitts, skates, tennis rackets, skis, balls of uncountable shapes and sizes: none of the stuff cluttering up American closets in the name of recreation has much usefulness beyond designated sporting purposes. Except, perhaps, for the baseball bat, a handy device for warding off assailants or intruders.

Yet the bike gets the Chinese commuter to and from work just as it gets Tony Rominger or Miguel Indurain around a track at 33 miles an hour or more. It transports the average American on zillions of small errands while also giving the kid a chance to scuff his or her knees trying to execute some new and nifty acrobatic trick. While a bike capable of breaking the one-hour record might come from the world of aerospace technology, made of exotic metals and adorned with all sorts of whiz-bang mechanical accoutrements, it's still pretty much the same basic machine as any other bike. It's still a two-wheeled vehicle with pedals and a chain for propulsion. Rominger and Indurain could still, if in need of a newspaper or a carton of milk, ride their record-breakers to the store and back.

Man and machine working together: Spaniard Miguel Indurain establishes a new record for the distance covered by a man on a bike in one hour—33 miles.

Indeed, such an ingenious invention is the bike that its design hasn't enormous front wheel and a small back wheel, a design predating the chain. But in fundamental form and concept, the pedal-powered two-wheeler has only been refined over the years, not radically redesigned or replaced by something better. Until some crafty inventor comes up with a human-powered hovercraft, or bionic roller skates, or some brilliant ergonomic device yet to be imagined, the bike remains the best and most versatile nonmotorized form of land transportation there is.

As much as it is a means of competing or exploring the world, the bicycle is a form of transportation—underutilized in the U.S.—for getting to and from work.

changed a whole heck of a lot since its evolutionary beginnings in the early 1800s. The name may have changed. The bicycle has been called, among other things, a velocipede, a velocar, and an ordinary, the name given to that nineteenth-century contraption with an

Still, for all of its basic sameness, the bike continues to be recast in many guises, and for many different purposes. That, too, is part of its beauty, the many variations schemed up around the two-wheeled theme.

While bikes come in all shapes and sizes, the basic elements—two wheels and pedals to propel you forward—are the same. Adherents of the recumbent bicycle insist it is the most efficient way to ride.

There is the mountain bike, the "hybrid" (or all-purpose) bike, the road-touring bike, the high-tech road-racing bike, the city bike, the BMX bike (short for bicycle motocross), the old three-speed with a bell and a kick-stand, the folding bike, the recumbent (a bike ridden in a reclining position, with legs horizontal rather than vertical), and so on. Inventors and bike builders march on in a never-ending search for the ideal correlation between design and function, or between design and performance, especially as new uses for a bike—mountain biking being the prime recent example—announce themselves.

Or just design for design's sake. The bike is a work of sculpture, make no mistake about it, and the existence of dozens of custom bike builders across the country is proof of that. The custom builders aren't in business to create bikes that are markedly better, performance-wise, than those churned out by factory-production companies. Their hand-welded creations instead find a place in this world on a level of art and craftsmanship rare in the development of recreational equipment. Look at the ordinaries of the nineteenth century; the stream-lined, atomic age roadsters of the 1950s; the wind-tunnel-tested racing machines for guys like Rominger and Indurain; the latest mountain bikes with their hydraulic suspension systems. Look at what's sitting in your own garage. Appreciate the crisply articulated

lines, the etched details, the interplay of color and metallic razzle-dazzle—it's sculpture wedding the aesthetic of Alexander Calder with the whimsy of Rube Goldberg. Bikes look cool. That's a big reason why people are enticed into buying them, even if they don't use them much thereafter.

Actually, a good many Americans do use their bikes, or at least say they do, more than might be imagined. According to recent surveys by the Bicycle Federation of America, more than 100 million Americans say they are bike riders. Not all ride very often; only about 31 million are adult riders who say they ride regularly. Yet the regular rider figure is roughly three times what it was in the early 1980s, an encouraging sign.

If there is one trend of recent years that is lifting more Americans off their sofas and onto their bike saddles it is mountain biking. Mountain biking has burst quickly upon the world of cycling—a legitimate and exciting new sport casting the playfulness of childhood stunt-riding against a backdrop of the rugged outdoors. Already it has established its own pantheon of stars to rival the likes of Indurain and Rominger: Jacquie Phelan, Julie Furtado, Missy Giove, Charlie Cunningham, Hans Rey, John Tomac. It will make its bow as an Olympic sport in Atlanta in 1996.

Approximately one of every three bikes sold in the United States is now a mountain bike (or at least classified as such), a category that constituted only about 5 percent of all sales in 1985. Take an old idea (the bike) and give it a sexy new spin (mountain biking), and suddenly America believes it has discovered a hot, new sport. Makes you wonder where the immortal old two-wheeler is headed next. Whitewater cycling? You never know.

According to the Bicycle Federation of America, 32 million Americans now ride mountain bikes. To be sure, most rarely, if ever, leave the pavement, suggesting that mountain biking is not reinventing cycling to the extent that its ardent adherents might want you to believe. But if simply the *image* of mountain biking—the sense of adventure, of recaptured youth—has been enough to get inactive riders back on two wheels, there is nothing wrong with that. Anything to get people riding. After all, millions of Americans who say they're bike riders still aren't riding very much.

Those irregulars represent the

DID YOU KNOW

The first person to cross North America on a bike was Thomas Stevens, who followed railroad tracks for much of his trip in 1884.

Moments and settings like this explain the explosion of interest in mountain biking. Since its invention in the early 80s, "fat tire" riding has revolutionized the industry and the sport.

Mountain biking has opened a new world for cyclists—one all but inaccessible on traditional road bikes.

substantial majority of riders, and maybe you are among them. So if you need reasons to get back in the saddle, here are five:

1) IT'S GREAT EXERCISE. Cycling burns calories. How many calories, of course, depends on how long and how hard you ride. World-class racers are caloric infernos, raging through as many as 8,000 calories in a day's ride of, say, 150 miles at 25 miles an hour. Presumably, you won't be so gung-ho, but in an hour's ride at 13 mph—a pretty poky pace, at least for road riding—you'd still go through about 650 calories. Many a dedicated cyclist will tell you that one of the great joys of a regular riding regimen is that it issues a license to eat without fear of pudginess. Also, cycling has tremendous cardiovascular benefits. Ed Burke, a leading cycling physiologist, says an *active* person can increase his or her aerobic capacity by as much as 25 percent by undertaking a well-planned training program. Imagine the increase possible for some sedentary lush.

2) IT'S EASY. You don't have to be athletic, coordinated, young, fit, smart, or good-looking to be a competent cyclist. You can *make* a ride hard if you want to, but you can also spend much of the time relaxing in the saddle, coasting, enjoying the scenery, chumming with friends.

3) YOU GET TO GO PLACES, SEE THE WORLD. Running is too slow, driving

too fast and too enclosed. Cycling—assuming you aren't blasting away in aerobic overdrive—moves at the pace of the poet: you get to look around, notice details in the shapes of trees, or the contours of the land, or the color of flowers, or the angular peculiarities of buildings, or the moods of people you pass. And that's just in riding around the block near home. Wait till you head out on a *real* ride.

Dead Horse Point near Moab, Utah. Is there a place on earth where a mountain bike and determined rider can't go?

4) YOU CAN DO IT WITH ANYBODY. You can ride with friends. You can ride with your children, five years old and up. You can ride with your grandparents. Bicycling can be the foundation of a great date; pack a picnic and go for a ride with the one you love or lust after. You can compete in races or enter any of the numerous "fun" rides organized by bike groups across the country. Cycling is America's great form of recreational inclusion.

5) YOU GET TO BE AN OUTRAGEOUS GEAR-NIK. Perhaps only fly fishing can rival cycling as a sport in which you can spend preposterous amounts of money for very insignificant things. You don't have to, of course; no obligation to buy, as is often said in sales come-ons. Yet serious cyclists, as they move deeper and deeper into their devotion to the sport, become lured to shiny, superlight equipment as cows are drawn to clover. High-end bike

gear is an extravagant and pleasurable addiction.

One other possibility: you might, in time, discover within yourself a latent aptitude for cycling—some deep aerobic and athletic gift that will lead you to challenging the one-hour record or becoming the first to ascend Mount Everest on a mountain bike. Maybe not. But the only way to find out what you're capable of as a cyclist is to get out there and do it.

Go for it.

Cycling, the sport for all ages: You're never too old or too young!

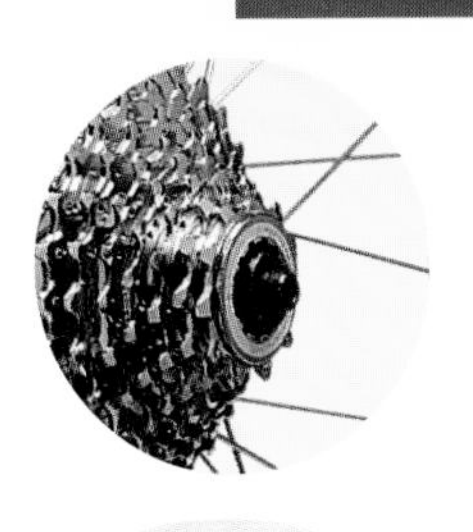

2 GEARING UP

To say that all bicycles are basically the same is akin to suggesting that there's little difference between a Dodge and a Ferrari. Yet both cars have four wheels and an engine, and both get you where you're going. Similarly, all bikes have two wheels, pedals, and a chain-propelled drivetrain. When foot pressure is applied to the pedals, all bikes move forward. It's no wonder, then, that cyclists keen on high performance find themselves fumbling for words in trying to explain the rationale for spending $3,000 on a bike. What does three grand buy that doesn't come in a basic $200 model? Like the Ferrari and the Dodge, don't both get you where you're going?

The answer, of course, is yes. But that's a "yes" tinged with deep shades of "no." No, as in there being no comparison between the $200 and $3,000 bike in terms of smoothness, speed, and efficiency of transportation. No, too, in terms of the relative effort required to make the klunker and the dream machine move forward.

Few sports can lure in equipment junkies the way cycling can, driving them up a price spiral in a spending frenzy. The fighter-jet metals, the lush paint, all those shiny parts . . . and then the bill. The klunker might hold you back in achieving your full cycling potential, but the high-end model can absolutely lay waste to your credit card balance.

Fortunately, there are hundreds of models between the two, allowing ample opportunity to find a satisfactory juncture between performance and price that suits your level of riding. But that broad array of models can also make the search for the ideal bike a confusing runaround. To restore order to the bike-buying process, you'll do well to stick with the original premise: all bikes are basically the same. Most bikes share six elements: frame, wheels, drivetrain, seat, handlebars, brakes. Using these six elements as bases for comparison should simplify your bike buying considerably.

ROAD BIKE ANATOMY

All bikes are essentially the same, consisting of frame, wheels, drivetrain, brakes, handlebars, and seat. Yet specialization makes one bike suited to touring on the open road, another to climbing mountain trails.

This Italian *Bianchi* road bike is designed for sustained riding on smooth, paved surfaces. The chief difference between it and a mountain bike (see pages 28 and 29) are handlebar design, wheel size and tire width, frame geometry, chain ring configuration, and overall weight. Notice that the triangle created by the frame is more open on a road bike, the seat tube is longer, the top tube is higher, and the bottom bracket and chain rings are lower.

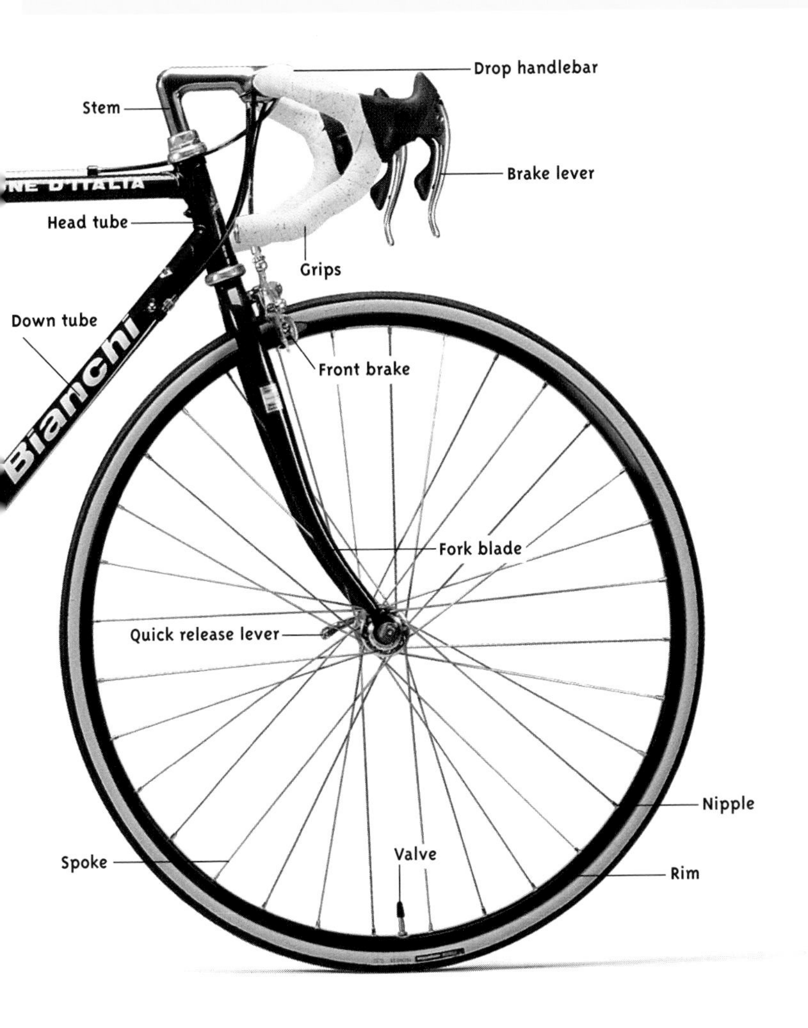

This high-end mountain bike sells for about $3,000 and sports a front suspension fork.

BASIC BUYING QUESTIONS

Why Buy?

Before making the bike-shop rounds, start by asking yourself the most basic question of all: why buy a bike? In other words, how do you plan to use the bike? More specifically, what type of roads or trails (paved or dirt, rough or smooth, flat or hilly, and so on) do you expect to ride?

This is crucial stuff, because the discouraging reality is that no bike is perfectly suited for all kinds of riding. The range of bike types you're likely to encounter in your shopping can probably be bracketed on one end by the sleek road-racing machine and on the other end by the full-bore mountain bike. (Price, at this point, is not an issue; you can spend a few hundred or thousands on almost any type of bike.) Each is designed for—and is great for—a very specific type of riding, but its performance plummets outside of its element.

The ascendancy of mountain biking in the 1990s has led many shop owners to crowd road bikes off their racks in favor of mountain bikes. Mountain bikes have a cachet, making them easier to sell. Yet true mountain bikes are less than ideal for many of the people buying them, particularly riders who rarely venture off paved roads. Just as the roadster flounders in negotiating unpaved rough stuff, the knobby-tired, small-framed, low-geared mountain bike is a relative sluggard on pavement.

Covering a broad middle ground between the extremes are so-called hybrids. Hybrids are suitable for riding on paved and unpaved surfaces, but they are by nature compromises. They are neither rugged enough to take on the pounding of strenuous, off-road mountain biking, nor are they a match for high-quality road bikes for long rides on pavement. Still, for the rider who regularly encounters a combination of paved and unpaved roads—and who doesn't demand the highest level of performance—the hybrid is an excellent option. In fact, hybrids and their closely related cousins, "utility" or "city" bikes, make great sense for

As a gathering place for riders, a clearinghouse of local cycling information, and a place for maintenance, advice, and riding tips, your local bike shop is much more than just a place to buy a bike.

commuting cyclists. They're functional, easy to operate, and moderately priced. And, just to confuse matters, they may be called mountain bikes by bike companies or shop owners still selling that mountain-biking cachet.

RIDING FREQUENCY. Next question: how often (as in how many hours or miles a week) do you expect to ride? If you expect to be only an occasional rider, shelling out serious money for a high-end machine would be a spendthrift indulgence. A bike costing less than $500 will do a very competent job of getting you where you're going. On the other hand, if you expect to be on your bike often, you'll come to appreciate—even bless—the more efficient performance of a better bike. Raising a final question: how insistent are you on high performance? The performance issue—the subtleties and minutiae of bike design and components that make one bike perform slightly better than another—is what really explains the quantum price gap between the $200 and $3,000 machines.

This is where the law of diminishing returns comes into play. The

$3,000 bike does not, quantifiably, increase cycling performance by a factor of 15 over the $200 bike. And each incremental increase in spending (you can, if so moved, spend considerably *more* than $3,000) produces less and less of a noticeable performance gain. Once the *serious* bike-buying zone has been entered—consider an arbitrary threshold to be $1,000—only the truly experienced or finicky rider can distinguish, or really care about, the performance gain represented by each increment of, say, $200. In fact, big spenders in the bike-buying game are probably motivated as much by snob appeal as by the quest for sublime cycling performance.

MOUNTAIN BIKE ANATOMY

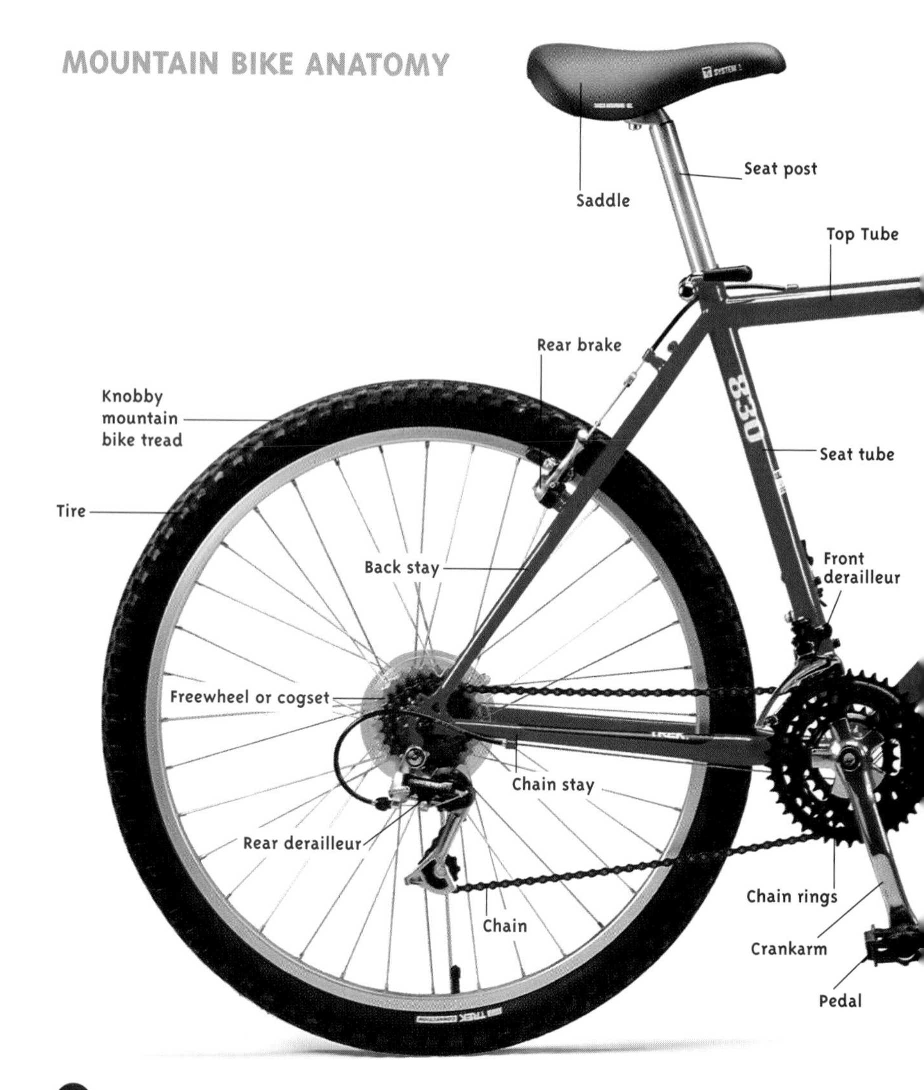

MOUNTAIN BIKE ANATOMY

This *TREK* mountain bike sports the fat, knobby tires of its species, along with more gears (note the three chain rings at the pedals), beefier cantilever brakes. Notice that compared to the road bike pictured on pages 24 and 25, the *TREK's* seat tube is shorter, its top tube lower, and its bottom bracket and chain ring are higher.

Now for specifics, the literal nuts and bolts of bike buying. Take each of the six basic components—frame, wheels, drivetrain, seat, handlebars, and brakes—and consider them in order.

THE FRAME

Frame Facts

If it weren't for a dazzling paint job and the fancy moving parts attached to it, a bike frame would lose much of its sex appeal. Metal tubing, on its own merits, is not particularly exciting. Yet the frame is the key element of any bike purchase, if for no better reason than the fact that it is the most expensive and so the least replaceable. You can always buy a better derailleur or new wheels or another crankset and install them in quick order. Replacing a frame is not so easy.

Expect two things from a well-built bike frame—responsiveness and lightness, in order of importance and somewhat related. The best way to understand what's meant by responsiveness is to feel it for yourself. Ask a bike-shop manager to allow you to briefly test ride a very inexpensive bike and a bike in, say, the $1,000 range. (Be sure to bring a photo I.D. and a credit card—a store owner might ask for them as collateral when you walk out of the shop with a high-priced bike—and if the shop staff aren't cooperative about allowing a test ride, shop elsewhere.) The expensive bike should jump forward with the first, slight push of the pedal and reach a cruising speed quickly and smoothly. By comparison, the low-end bike will seem lackluster in responding to that initial pedal push, and more effort will be required to get it to (and keep it at) cruising speed.

The difference in responsiveness is due primarily to a difference in the frame metals and the different way the tubing is bonded together. Here lightness makes its entrance: bikes made of lighter metals tend to be more responsive simply because they present less of a load for you to push around.

Unfortunately, a test ride in a parking lot probably won't help much in distinguishing the differences in the responsiveness of two comparably priced bikes. You would need to ride them for many miles over varying terrain for significant differences to become apparent. To have at least *some* idea of which bikes within your price range might be most responsive for your kind of riding, you ought to know a few things about the way frames are designed and built.

Frame Design

Most bike frames are configured around the main triangle formed by a bike's three largest tubes—the seat tube, the top tube, and the down tube. This configuration is referred to as a bike's "geometry," and decades of design experimentation have gone into calculating the performance effects of varying the angles of that geometry by as little as half a degree. The result of all that design tinkering? The angles on almost all road frames and hybrids fall within a very narrow range of only about three degrees. In fact, the basic angles vary only slightly from the geometry of adult tricycles developed in the 1880s. You'll encounter somewhat more variation in mountain-bike frames. That might be because mountain biking, as a discrete form of recreation, is still in its adolescence, its roots reaching back only to the late 1970s. As riders continue to push the limits of the sport, as they take on terrain unimaginable even a few years ago, frame design continues to be reworked.

Michael Gabrick near Evanston, Wyoming, on his coast-to-coast highwheel ride. This modern model is a direct descendant of nineteenth century bikes.

Even so, the vast majority of mountain-bike frames still feature geometry very similar to road-bike frames. Look for one noteworthy difference, however. On a frame built for really rugged off-road riding, the bottom bracket—where the pedal crank arms are attached (see "Mountain Bike Anatomy," pages 28–29)—is higher than on a road frame, the added height providing extra clearance over obstacles along the trail. Also, a mountain bike's triangle is usually smaller than that of a touring bike or hybrid.

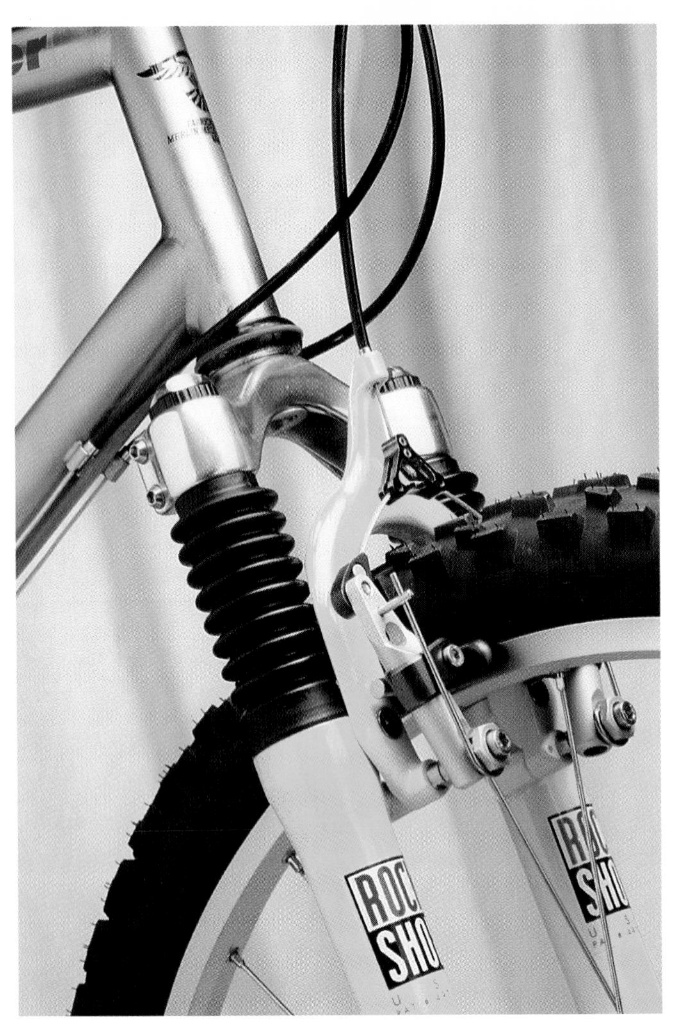

Many mountain bikes now sport suspension systems on the front fork to absorb some of the bumps of the trail; they retail for upwards of $500.

That adds structural rigidity to stand up to the roughness of the terrain. It also makes the bike more maneuverable in tight spots.

Tighter frame geometry generally results in a stiffer, less flexible bike. Conversely, more "open" geometry generally results in a slightly more elastic, softer-riding frame.

The Fork

A bike's relative stiffness or elasticity is also affected by the fork, the pronged piece of tubing that holds the front wheel to the frame. The *angle* at which the fork projects downward from the head tube and the fork's "rake"—its relative amount of curvature—also help determine a bike's wheelbase. The steeper the angle and the less the rake (or, the straighter the fork) the shorter the wheelbase and the stiffer the ride.

The fork angle and rake also affect a bike's steering, because a lower, or shallower, angle, which projects the front wheel farther ahead, generally makes a bike easier to steer. That's why mountain bikes often have shallower fork angles than many road bikes, ease of steering being a more critical factor when bouncing around off-road.

Fully suspended mountain bikes like this Mountain Cycle, with suspension built into the fork, frame, and seat, are the latest rage in mountain biking. They also carry a considerable price tag, starting around $3,000. Notice, also, the disk brakes on this model.

Frame Suspension

Speaking of bouncing around . . . the current rage in mountain-bike design is "suspension"—shock-absorption systems designed to take some of the roughness out of that bouncy ride. The most common place to find suspension devices or shock absorbers is in the fork, but many manufacturers offer full-suspension models, with shock absorbers built into the bottom bracket or rear stays.

Unless you're going to spend a lot of time taking on the rough off-road stuff, the extra expense of shock-absorbing suspension systems may not make sense. Although you can find bikes in the $500 range with fork suspension, dual-suspension bikes range from about $1,000 to over $4,000. A few of the world's top competitive mountain bikers still prefer bikes without suspension. Their thinking is that suspension is largely superfluous if your riding technique is honed and your anticipation of the terrain ahead is keen.

FRAME MATERIALS

Steel

Less expensive bikes are made with thick-walled segments of steel tubing. Not only is the metal heavier than on more expensive frames, it has little built-in resilience or spring to it. More expensive steel frames are built with thinner-walled (hence lighter) tubing that is usually "double-butted"—thicker at the ends—to add strength in the areas where the tubes are joined together. Steel alloys (a mix of metals

DID YOU KNOW
How far the ultra-light titanium craze has gone? How about titanium spokes, at about $3 a spoke.

such as chrome, manganese, and molybdenum) remain the materials of choice even for many high-priced frames. Steel is durable, responsive, and relatively easy for frame builders to work with. But lighter materials, notably aluminum and titanium, have begun nudging out steel alloys in the higher price brackets.

Aluminum

For most cyclists, a steel frame still represents perhaps the best meshing of economy and performance. If you're really set on getting a lighter-than-steel bike—but not eager to part with the mega-bucks necessary to buy a titanium frame—consider aluminum. The benefits of lightness can really pay off if your typical riding involves a lot of hill climbing.

Many avid cyclists, however, remain dubious about the structural muscle of aluminum to stand up to rugged, hard riding. Frame builders have tried to answer that concern by building aluminum frames with tubing much "fatter" (that is, tubes with a greater circumference) than the tubing on steel frames. This fat tubing is supposed to be as strong as a narrower steel tube. Another common concern about aluminum is that it is, by nature, less resilient than steel, often resulting in a stiffer ride. Nevertheless, aluminum frames have become very popular among riders who appreciate its combination of lightness and affordability.

Other Materials

Carbon fiber is a relatively new building material that has begun to creep into the middle price range. It may yet be a terrific solution to the performance-economy conundrum, but it has yet to establish a track record to prove itself over the long haul. Then there is titanium, currently the hot material in high-end frame construction. Highly responsive, light as aluminum, stronger than steel. And astonishingly expensive, as much as $3,000 for the frame alone.

The Bicycle Institute of America, citing the lessening of Cold War tensions, has speculated that the freeing up of tons of titanium from military applications may result in lower titanium prices for recreational uses. Maybe, but don't count on it. For all but the most dedicated or competitive riders, titanium frames remain a luxury. Unless you've got very deep pockets, it's hard to go wrong sticking with steel.

FRAME FITTING

The Straddle Method

"Without fit," says Richard Sachs, one of the foremost custom frame builders in the United States, a new bike "is worthless." That might sound like an exaggeration, but it's not: A good fit is the key to comfortable, efficient riding.

The first step in determining how well a bike fits you is to straddle it. For a road bike, the top tube should be about an inch below crotch level when your feet are flat on the floor. Mountain bikes are generally sized smaller, both for the added structural stability of a smaller frame and for added clearance above the top tube as your body moves around in negotiating variable and tricky terrain. For a mountain bike, allow about three to four inches between the top tube and your crotch. Many mountain bikes have top tubes angling downward toward the rear stays, in which case you should take your straddle measurement standing just in front of the seat.

Fine-Tuning a Fit

That's the quick and simple sizing method, one inevitably complicated by human anatomy. The fact is, riders come in all shapes and sizes. Some people with long legs have short arms, others have short legs and long arms. Riding styles and preferred riding postures vary widely. Just because a bike passes muster on the straddle test doesn't guarantee a good fit once you're on the road.

Any bike-shop salesperson worth his or her salary should be adept at matching you with a bike that suits your unique body shape. If a salesperson acts disinterested or clueless about fitting, you're shopping in the wrong place. Plenty of shops put a good deal of time, effort, and pride into assuring good fits. A few high-end shops specialize in custom fits, using a stationary mock frame on which the size and geometry can be adjusted. A

HOW TO MEASURE A BIKE

Have you ever said, "I have a 27-inch bike"? While your wheels might indeed be 27 inches across, chances are good that your *frame* size is not 27 inches. Although you may think of the size of your bicycle wheel as being the same as the size of your bike, your bike's frame size is not measured by the size of your wheels.

Bicycle frames are typically measured from the center of the seat tube to the center of the bottom bracket (aka "center-to-center") or from the top of the seat tube to the center of the bottom bracket (aka "center-to-top"). These measurements might be in centimeters or inches. Typically, the range for these measures is from 18 inches to 24 inches for road bikes and 14 inches to 18 inches for mountain bikes. (The corresponding ranges in centimeters are 48 cm to 62 cm, and 36 cm to 36 cm.)

The importance of a fine-tuned fit can't be overemphasized, and quality bike shops have fitting stands like this one. A fitting charge of $50 may be waived if you buy an expensive model. Ask your shop fitter for your dimensions, in case you want to buy another bike elsewhere.

charge—$50 or so—may be assessed for that service, but if you anticipate spending a lot of time in the saddle or have a hard-to-fit body (for example, especially short arms or legs), that may be $50 brilliantly spent.

THE WHEELS

In a 1956 article in *Cycling* magazine, L. Bruce Archer wrote, "Probably the strongest man-made structure relative to its weight is the bicycle wheel." The bike wheel, Archer reported, was able to sustain forces of up to 700 times its weight. Pretty amazing, which is probably why—despite attempts to improve upon it—the spoked wheel remains the standard for bikes four decades later.

Fat or Skinny?

But those marvelously sturdy spoked wheels do come in different circumferences and widths. Your wheel choice will essentially be determined by the type of bike you buy. Mountain bikes have wider wheel rims (ergo, wider tires) and smaller circumferences; road bikes have skinnier wheel rims and slightly larger circumferences; hybrids, as is their intrinsic character, combine elements of both.

The skinny wheels on road bikes are wonderful for riding on pavement, for a couple of reasons. One is that skinnier tires mean a smaller contact area and thus less friction between tire and road. Also, skinnier tires can be inflated to higher pressures—in some cases as high as 120 pounds per square inch (psi)—further reducing friction. You work less when there is less friction to work against.

But once off the pavement, skinny tires become problematic, skidding off rocks and literally becoming stuck in the mud. On dirt, sand, rock, and mud, friction becomes an ally, recasting itself as traction and stability. Better traction is the whole idea behind the fat, deeply treaded tires you'll find on mountain bikes. Mountain-bike tires usually can't be inflated much above 70 pounds, and for extra traction in very loose surfaces such as sand, mountain bikers sometimes reduce tire pressure to as low as 25 psi.

Fortunately, a change of tires—especially on mountain bikes and hybrids, for which tread options are greater than for road bikes—is relatively easy. If you plan to do much riding on unpaved surfaces, go with wider, deeper tires. If you're going to be riding smoother surfaces, look for smoother, friction-resistant tires. You can always switch from a smooth tread

Smooth treads are best for smooth surfaces where they create a minimum of drag. Deeply grooved, knobby treads provide extra traction on tough terrain. Hybrid bikes are equipped with a compromise between the two.

DID YOU KNOW

French existentialist Jean-Paul Sartre had this to say about cycling in his book, *Being and Nothingness:* "Handing over a bank note is enough to make a bicycle belong to me, but my entire life is needed to realize this possession."

GEAR TALK

EXTRA WHEELS

An investment you might also want to consider at some point in your cycling life is an extra set of wheels. Racers often have one set of training wheels—a set they don't mind roughing up a little—and a set of wheels they reserve in perfect shape just for racing. Mountain bikers often have a set of wheels for especially rough conditions and another set for smoother riding. Two sets of wheels don't make sense for everybody; at $150 and up, an extra set of wheels is probably not a wise investment for someone riding a $200 bike. But if you've sunk $1,000 or more in a bike, extra wheels to make your bike more versatile might make good sense. They're cheaper than buying a whole new bike.

to a deep tread, or vice versa, if the surface conditions call for it.

THE DRIVETRAIN

There are five parts here: the crankset, the pedals, the freewheel or cogset, the chain, and the gear-shifting mechanism, usually comprising front and rear derailleurs.

One of the nice things about this multiplicity of moving parts is that you don't have to settle for any particular setup. Of course, you want to be sure that all of the drivetrain components that your new bike is equipped with work, especially the shifting mechanisms. But it is relatively easy, and not outlandishly expensive, to replace the pedals, the freewheel or cogset (the cluster of cogs on the rear wheel), the chain, or chain rings on the crankset (the combination, at the front of the drivetrain, of chain rings and crankarms).

The two drivetrain elements to focus on initially are the pedals and the gear setup. The foot-to-pedal juncture is the critical contact point in the man-and-machine bonding. If you are at all interested in efficient riding—in lessening your workload and increasing your performance—you'll want to do all you can to solidify that bond. That means, at the very least, investing in toe clips, those curved metal (or plastic) contraptions attached to the pedal.

The Pedals

Riders unaccustomed to toe clips often find them a cumbersome annoyance. They never quite get the hang of kicking the pedal over to get the foot properly positioned under the clip. But toe clips perform an invaluable function: they keep the foot properly positioned on the pedal throughout the pedaling stroke. (They are not, incidentally, for pulling the pedal up on

The drivetrain: pedals connected to the crankset connected to the chain rings connected to the chain connected to the cogset connected to the rear hub. Notice the three chain rings, mark of a mountain bike's many gears.

with toe clips; plus, cleated shoes don't make great walking shoes.

The Gears

The gear setup is, again, something you can change relatively easily, so don't feel you're stuck with what you start with. The main thing you should be looking for initially is the range of gears. In

the back side of the stroke. Ergonomic studies of professional cyclists using toe clips have shown that experienced cyclists do not use the clips in this way.) Thanks to toe clips, foot and pedal move in sync, not to be disrupted by rough road surfaces or erratic leg movements.

A better, albeit more expensive, way to maximize the foot/pedal bond is a unified pedal/shoe cleat system. (See "Shoes" in Chapter 3.) A cleat on the bottom of the shoe snaps onto a pedal specially designed to receive it. These systems are not only a more effective way than toe clips of keeping the foot in place, they are also easier to get in and out of than toe clips. All racers and most high-performance riders use this kind of pedal system. The disadvantages are 1) the extra expense, and 2) a bike equipped with these special pedals is almost impossible to ride without shoes rigged up with the proper cleats. In short, they're more efficient but less versatile than pedals

DID YOU KNOW

Cyclists spend hundreds — even thousands — of dollars to trim weight off their bikes and hundreds of hours to trim weight off their bodies. That's why the P.I.G.G. Cycling-Specific Weight Trainer is surely one of the most ridiculous ideas to hit the cycling scene in years. Basically it's a water bottle filled with cement that comes in dumb (6.6 pounds), dumber (11 pounds), and dumbest (13.2 pounds) versions. Put one in your bottle cage and make your bike heavier and your riding more strenuous. Great idea, huh?

assessing that range on a prospective purchase, you need to know the gear fundamentals.

Higher gears propel a bike farther with each pedal stroke, but higher gears are also harder to pedal. In a lower gear, you will cover a shorter distance with each stroke, but your pedaling will be easier. The bigger the cogs on the rear wheel, the smaller the gear. The bigger the chain ring on the crankset, the bigger the gear. And in both cases, of course, the converse is true: smaller in back means a bigger gear; smaller in front means smaller gear.

Most road bikes have two chain rings on the crankset, while mountain bikes usually have three chain rings.

Advanced riders tend to prefer "clipless" systems (below), in which a cleat on the shoe snaps into a pedal specifically designed to accept it, locking the foot into the proper position at all times. Toe clips (above) also secure the foot in position, though not as reliably as clipless systems.

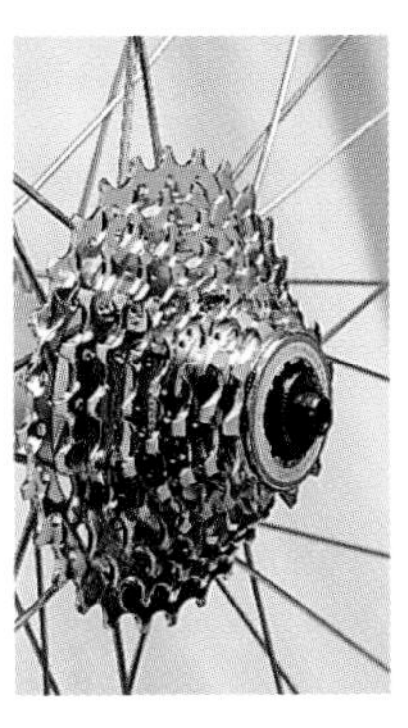

The road bike cogset (left) has 7 cogs, while the mountain bike cogset (right) has 8 cogs. The mountain bike cogs are also larger, for lower gears to climb steep hills.

The extra chain ring on the mountain bike adds very low gears for the kind of steep, rough climbing that road bikes usually aren't subjected to. Rear wheels have up to eight cogs. Do the math and you come up with a possible maximum of 24 gears.

Are 24 gears necessary? The answer is, in a word, no—although perhaps half of all mountain bikes come with that many gears as standard equipment. More gears make for smoother shifting and narrow the increments between gears, to the point where the incremental differences are almost indistinguishable. More gears might add shifting versatility, but they don't necessarily increase your shifting range—that is, the range between your highest and lowest gears. Also, a few of those gears are all but useless, notably the combination of the smallest chain ring in front and the smallest cogwheel in back. When the gears are shifted in this position, the chain tends to grind against the gear teeth, rather than engage smoothly, thereby hindering your performance.

The one gear to be particularly mindful of in the setup on your new bike is the lowest gear (smallest ring up front, biggest cog on the back). That's the gear you'll need for climbing steep hills. In its guidelines for touring cyclists, the Adventure Cycling Association—the well-respected, nonprofit touring organization—recommends a chain ring of between 24 and 28 teeth in front and a cogwheel in back with between 30 and 34 teeth. The rule here is: when in doubt, go smaller. Climbing with a gear too big is tortuous going, whereas spinning a gear that might be too small simply means getting to the hilltop will take longer.

Remember that you can easily adapt your gear setup to your riding. Many experienced cyclists have two or more freewheels (freewheels start at around $20) with different gear ratios. They'll simply change freewheels to match the hilliness of the terrain they expect to encounter. It is also very easy to change gear rings on a cogset, the variation on the freewheel with

DID YOU KNOW

One of the latest gadgets for the compleat cyclist is a plastic case, which can be mounted on the handlebars or behind the seat, to carry a cellular telephone.

which many new bikes are now equipped.

Aero bars allow road riders to maintain a low, aerodynamic position over the long haul, but when using them, you sacrifice steering and braking control.

THE SEAT

Irregular or occasional cyclists are inclined to prefer wider and softer saddles. Give 'em lots of cushion and spring—a virtual lounge chair on wheels. Well, if you *were* just lounging around, the wide, soft saddle would be great, but it's not the best design for efficient riding. The wide saddle interferes with the movement of your legs and increases the likelihood of uncomfortable chafing on your inner legs. In addition, the soft, bouncy saddle lessens your leverage in delivering full, even strokes to the pedals.

For performance-minded cyclists, men and women, a relatively rigid saddle is the best choice. It might take some time to adjust the saddle positioning to suit your riding style, but once you hit on the perfect position, and once you and your saddle become acquainted, you're unlikely to think twice about what you're sitting on.

Of course, no cyclist, no matter how performance conscious, wants to be stuck with an uncomfortable seat. If you're only an occasional rider, not putting in the mileage necessary to adapt to the saddle, a good choice would be a saddle with a built-in gel layer. The gel provides a thin, comforting cushion between bone and hard saddle surface, but it doesn't have the bounciness of a heavily cushioned or spring-loaded saddle. There are also saddles specifically designed for women. These are slightly wider than the classic racing saddle—an acknowledgment of the anatomical difference between women and men.

THE HANDLEBARS

Road bikes usually have "drop bars"—handlebars elegantly curved to resemble sleek, metallic ram's horns. Mountain bikes and hybrids are usually equipped with straight handlebars. Drop bars are an ingenious design, their primary advantage being that they allow you to sit low on the bike in a streamlined, aerodynamic position. Yet they also allow you to grip the bars in three or four different positions. Being able to shift your hand position means being able to shift your *body* position. That shifting helps to rest arm and neck muscles and relieve back stress, a big bonus on a long ride.

Unfortunately, most riders never figure out how to best put drop bars to use, and the beauty of the design goes unappreciated. That is one reason why most new bikes now have straight (or more or less straight) handlebars: they're easier to figure out and easier to get used to. The resulting upright body position might not be aerodynamic, but it does help provide stability and improved steering leverage.

All mountain bikes have straight bars, since steering control is much

Giro

more important than aerodynamics when the going gets rough. Some mountain bikers also add bar ends, which are adjustable extensions that allow the mountain biker, like a road rider, to vary hand (and riding) positions to relieve stress. That's an option worth considering, but also one that, in most cases, you'll have to pay extra for.

Side-pull brakes, light and easy to adjust, are common on road bikes.

THE BRAKES

Bicycle brakes are pretty straightforward. The main difference between expensive and inexpensive brakes is the weight of the construction materials. One important variation on the basic brake theme, however, is brakes bolted to pivots on the fork and rear stays on many mountain bikes. This design provides extra braking stability—and reliability—when riding rugged terrain. If you expect to do a lot of off-pavement riding, it's a design feature you'll appreciate.

GEAR TALK

AERO BARS

Sales of so-called aero bars surged after Greg LeMond used them in his dramatic, final day ride to win the 1989 Tour de France. LeMond nipped Frenchman Laurent Fignon, riding without aero bars, by eight seconds. Extending forward from standard handlebars and usually with cushioned rests for the forearms, aero bars allow riders to maintain a low, aerodynamic position. For long, hard rides, they're great, relieving strain on the back, shoulder, and arm muscles while reducing wind drag dramatically. But their use is limited. You sacrifice steering and braking control, making aero bars a bad idea for riding in traffic or in groups and a ridiculous idea for backcountry mountain biking. Several models are available as clip-ons that attach to standard handlebars; you can mount them and remove them as needed. If you expect to do a lot of solo riding on the road, aero bars are a good investment. Otherwise, plunking down up to $150 for aero bars is a waste of money.

Cantilever brakes, anchored to fork blades (shown) and back stays for extra braking stability, are common on mountain bikes.

Advanced roller-cam brakes, found on some high-end mountain bikes, provide peak mechanical advantage.

UPGRADING

After riding your new bike for a while, you might decide that it's time for an upgrade. You might realize, for example, that your performance would improve considerably with clipless pedals (if you're riding with toe clips), new tires or wheels, or different gearing. New pedals and gearing can make you a more efficient rider, a new saddle can make you a more comfortable rider, new tires or wheels can help you adapt to the specific terrain on which you like to ride. There are plenty of good reasons to upgrade your bike's components.

Still, upgrading is a process to approach warily. In most cases, higher-end components and accessories don't function markedly better than less expensive counterparts; they're simply lighter. It is absolutely flabbergasting how much can be spent to pare a few measly grams from the overall weight of a bike. A pair of titanium "skewers," for example—the quick-release rods that run through the wheel axles and hold the wheels to the bike—runs about $70. The weight saved is an all but inconsequential few grams. While almost all riders ride with steel chains, running between $6 and $20 or so, it's possible to shell out $375 for a titanium chain and pare a few more grams from the overall weight of your bike.

Shape Up Before Spending

So go ahead—spend yourself silly in upgrading to ultralight components or on ultralight accessories. Yet for all but the most fit riders, there's a much cheaper and more sensible route to weight savings: get in shape. Get a good, responsive, moderately priced bike, and ride off those few extra

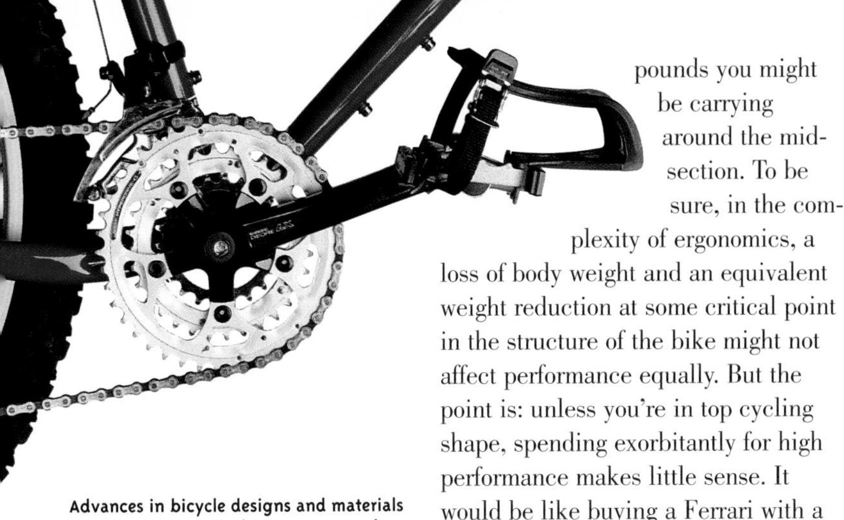

Advances in bicycle designs and materials really add up to one thing: greater, safer thrills on two wheels.

pounds you might be carrying around the midsection. To be sure, in the complexity of ergonomics, a loss of body weight and an equivalent weight reduction at some critical point in the structure of the bike might not affect performance equally. But the point is: unless you're in top cycling shape, spending exorbitantly for high performance makes little sense. It would be like buying a Ferrari with a Dodge engine.

THE BUYING GAME

What do you get for your money? Here is an approximate breakdown of what's what in very general price categories.

$200 AND UNDER—Klunkerville. Bikes in this range are adequate for basic transportation (for example, running errands), but their performance weaknesses will become apparent on rides much longer than 5 miles. Don't go knocking klunkers; the original mountain bikes of the 1970s would have fit proudly in this category. While you can probably expect a frame built solidly enough to smash unscathed through a brick wall, you should make sure that brakes and derailleurs work smoothly. For kids' bikes, of course, this is obviously an appropriate range. But even for a minimal level of recreational or sporting performance, it's worth chipping in the extra bucks for something better.

$200-$500—Ironically, as you move up the pricing ladder, less costs more. The frame tubing becomes lighter, as do the components. In terms of weight savings, you're already making a significant step up from Klunkerville. Still, relatively heavy steel, for the frame tubing, components, and wheel rims, is the primary structural element. For the cyclist who only occasionally embarks on rides of more than 20 miles, but regularly takes spins of 8 to 10 miles, this is a good price range to consider.

continued on page 48

THE BUYING GAME

continued from page 47

$500-$1,000—A true performance machine begins coming together within this range. Expect frames to be built of light, responsive steel alloy tubing or of even lighter aluminum. Expect components that look and perform very similarly to components you'll find on the most expensive bikes. Beyond this price zone, the performance curve begins to level off sharply. Small increases in performance potential and decreases in overall weight start costing serious bucks. This is the price range where most active recreational cyclists will probably get the most for their money.

ABOVE $1,000—You're now in the price range of the committed or competitive cyclist. At this point, you should be getting picky and have a pretty focused idea of what you're looking for. You want to be sure you're getting more frame for your money, not just a moderately priced frame dolled up with more expensive components. Remember that it's much easier (and less expensive) to upgrade components than to buy a new frame. At this point you should also be looking into a clipless pedal system, to be sure to make the most of the extra performance you've invested in. If you plan to ride regularly—three or more times a week—and you live and ride in hilly country, you might really do yourself a favor to jump up to this price range. Lightness and frame responsiveness really show their worth when going uphill.

WAY ABOVE $1,000—Welcome to the obsession zone. You are now looking at frames made of exotic materials—titanium, boron, magnesium, ceramic compounds, carbon fiber—that alone can cost $2,000 or more. Wheels and components to outfit the frame can easily run another $2,000. You are starting to think in terms of grams vs. dollars. A component (let's say brake levers) will pare another 15 grams from your overall bike weight yet will cost an extra $200, and you figure it's worth it. In the obsession zone, cycling can become a hazard to your financial well-being.

3 CLOTHING

If your heart were set on it, you could ride a bike stark naked. It is not a recommended procedure, of course, particularly in communities that look on public exposure disapprovingly. But the point is—theoretically if impractically—that no special attire is necessary to ride a bike.

How ironic it is, then, that cycling may lead the world of sport and recreation in its unabashed trumpeting of a sport-specific, aerobic "look." The often dazzling colors of cycling attire, the form-fitting sheen of Lycra shorts, the sexy shades—the "compleat" cyclist tends to be a streamlined, Technicolor fashion statement. Cyclists regularly dress up in ways that, if it weren't for the fact that they were cyclists, would be embarrassing (not to mention awkward or uncomfortable) even at a masquerade party. Yet once the cyclist is astride a bike, this peculiar dress is accepted as perfectly normal.

Cycling attire combines three elements: function, fashion, and advertisement. The first, of course, is most important and the second purely a matter of choice. The third has evolved in a way that must surprise even the purveyors of products pitched by the endorsements on cycling clothing. Cycling shirts and shorts are regularly—and loudly—adorned with product names and logos, usually representing the sponsors of major bike-racing teams.

Among committed bike tourers, nearly any outfit will do in a pinch. Ideally, a snug-fitting rain slicker to reduce wind resistance would be best.

Indeed, product billboarding on cycling attire has risen to a high level of fashion art form, and corporate marketeers must be overjoyed to see people who have *paid* to wear clothing that lavishly advertises their products.

You don't, of course, have to advertise anybody's anything to dress well for cycling. But what *do* you need? In order of importance, a proper-fitting helmet is essential; a good pair of shoes and shorts almost as essential; and shirt and sport-specific eyewear optional though probably helpful.

HELMET

More and more states now have laws requiring young cyclists to wear helmets. In California, for example, the helmet law applies to riders eighteen and under. Helmet laws for kids have a statistical rationale: approximately three of every four bicycling head injuries involve kids fifteen and under. (Such a rationale, incidentally, ought to lead to laws requiring men to wear helmets, since almost three of every four bike accidents involve men.) Yet adults can still do as they please, and most cyclists—more than 90 percent—choose to ride helmetless. So go ahead and be like them. This being a country where liberty is cherished, you are free to be stupid. Chances are you'll survive.

Yet survival chances are far better

Cyclists come in all looks and sizes. Pick whatever look suits you, as long as you wear a helmet at all times.

if you do wear a helmet. In a study of bicycling head injuries, reported in the *Journal of the American Medical Association,* Dr. Jeffrey Sacks estimated that as many as 2,500 of 2,985 deaths and 757,000 of 905,752 head injuries could have been prevented had riders been wearing helmets. "One death could have been prevented every day [of the period studied], and one head injury could have been prevented every four minutes," Sacks concluded.

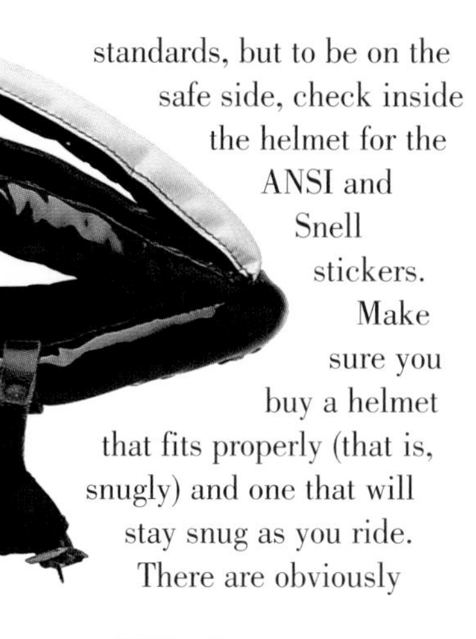

Proper Fit

Start by considering only helmets designed specifically for cycling. Something like a hockey helmet or a ski-racing helmet won't do. The reasons? Cycling helmets are designed in consideration of the types of falls, and the resulting cranial impacts, that are unique to cycling. In this regard, cycling helmets should pass the standards of either the American National Standards Institute (ANSI) or the Snell Memorial Foundation, preferably both. It is unlikely that any helmet you'll find in any bike shop is *not* up to both standards, but to be on the safe side, check inside the helmet for the ANSI and Snell stickers.

Make sure you buy a helmet that fits properly (that is, snugly) and one that will stay snug as you ride. There are obviously

Old fashioned leather strap helmets (1) are not up to modern ANSI and Snell safety standards. Hard-shelled helmets with visors (2) are acceptable, especially for lower-speed touring, but not as good as the crushed Styrofoam helmets (3) designed to break on impact. More expensive helmets (4 and 5) feature aerodynamic contouring and more ventilation.

This is one way to bring a child along on a ride, but a molded-plastic, rear-mounted child seat would provide better protection. Whatever your choice, a helmet is a must; about 3 out of every 4 bicycling head injuries involve kids 15 years old and younger.

many different head shapes, and so there are many different helmet shapes. Since helmets are easy enough to try on, try on more than one model, and in more than one size, to find what best suits your noggin. Helmet manufacturers often include movable and removable pads to improve snugness, but think of the pads as fine-tuning devices, not filler material to compensate for what's basically a lousy fit.

When you've found a helmet that feels right, it's worth taking a two-minute ride around the block to find out how it might shift on your head in various riding positions. A shifty helmet can be not only uncomfortable but risky. Helmets are generally designed to be worn well over the forehead, within a couple of inches of the eyebrows. Sometimes, helmets have a tendency to drift backward because of the way cyclists cock their heads when riding in a forward-leaning position. That drift—which can lessen the effectiveness of the helmet in certain types of falls—can be minimized by cinching the helmet straps. But if the drift can't be corrected through strap-cinching, try a different model.

Price Questions

You can spend as little as $25 for a helmet, and you can spend more than $100. The most expensive helmets are generally designed with racing or high-performance cycling in mind, and so may be designed to withstand impacts resulting from falls in situations—descending a steep hill at over 50 miles an hour, for instance—that the typical recreational cyclist is unlikely to encounter. In other words, for certain unusual situations, a more expensive helmet might be safer. Yet in terms of passing the basic ANSI and Snell standards, and thus for almost all riding conditions, the $25 helmet and the $100-plus helmet are both acceptable.

Usually one of the benefits of a more expensive helmet is lightness. A few extra ounces on your head might not seem like much if you're only out for an easy 15- or 20-minute ride. But a lighter helmet can make a difference on a longer, more strenuous ride. When a cyclist is in a normal riding position, with the back angled, the weight of the head gets less support from the body than in a straight-up standing position. In other words, your neck and upper-back muscles do extra work to keep your head from falling right onto the handlebars. A lighter helmet is a way of lessening the load those muscles must bear.

More expensive helmets generally feature better ventilation, another factor that becomes increasingly important the more you ride. And finally, more expensive helmets generally have better aerodynamic design, something that's probably not too important unless you plan on racing regularly or unless it's important to you to make a fashion statement about the ultimate in streamlined cool.

Adjust your cinch straps to make sure your helmet fits snugly and sits low over your forehead.

Yes, fashion does come into play in picking a helmet. After all, one of the main reasons cyclists *don't* wear helmets is the fear of looking dorky. Indeed, when cycling-specific hard-shelled helmets first began proliferating in the late 1970s, the dorky look of the plain white half shell was a turnoff for a lot of riders. But helmet design has come a long way since, in terms of fashion as well as fit and safety. The only dorky-looking riders these days are those who haven't taken the time to shop for the helmet that's right for them.

One last note: many helmets are actually designed to break on impact.

This is a way of dissipating the contact force between your skull and the ground. Many helmet manufacturers will replace cracked helmets free of charge. In fact Giro, a leading helmet maker, reports that it replaces up to 5,000 helmets a year, an indication that plenty of helmets are serving their protective purpose.

SHOES

You see it all too often—a cyclist who has invested $1,000 or more in a high-performance bike and is pedaling it with sneakers. Simply put, that sneakered rider is not getting his or her money's worth. An inadequate pair of shoes weakens the bike-and-rider bond by short-circuiting the efficient transfer of energy from cyclist to cycle. Put another way, improper shoes mean more work.

Cycling shoes start at around $50 and can cost more than $200. All models, however, are characterized by a single critical feature: a rigid sole. Here, in a biomechanical nutshell, is why: the ball of your foot, the contact point with a bicycle pedal, is forward of the ankle, where leg and foot come together. Nature cleverly concocted this design because it works ideally for walking, an activity that requires flexibility from toe to heel.

The Rigid Sole

Nature didn't account for human beings coming up with a clever design of their own: the bicycle. The leg-and-foot configuration is less than ideal for cycling: when you push down on the pedal with your leg, much of the downward force is directed behind the ball of the foot. Enter a very simple solution: the rigid sole. The rigid sole provides the leveraging platform to transmit efficiently the energy from the downward push of the leg to the ball of the foot and thus to the pedal.

There is a drawback, more practical than biomechanical. Rigid-soled shoes are lousy for walking. Some of the higher-end racing shoes—not only with rigid soles but also with peculiarly contoured soles to further maximize energy transfer—are all but impossible to walk in for more than a few feet. And any "clipless" pedal system—in which cleats on the bottoms of your shoes snap into specially designed pedals—make walking unusually hard. Ironically, then, your first consideration in buying a pair of cycling shoes is this: how much time in your cycling life do you expect *not* to be riding?

If, on a typical ride, you expect to be off your bike often and walking around, taking hikes, or running errands, go for a touring shoe or a mountain-biking shoe. In look and design, these shoes don't vary greatly from a walking or running shoe except for that one, critical element: the rigid sole. (Some of these shoes may be compromises, sacrificing some rigidity to make walking easier.) On many of these shoes, the cleats—should you have a clipless-pedal system—are recessed in the sole to further facilitate walking. If, on the other hand, your

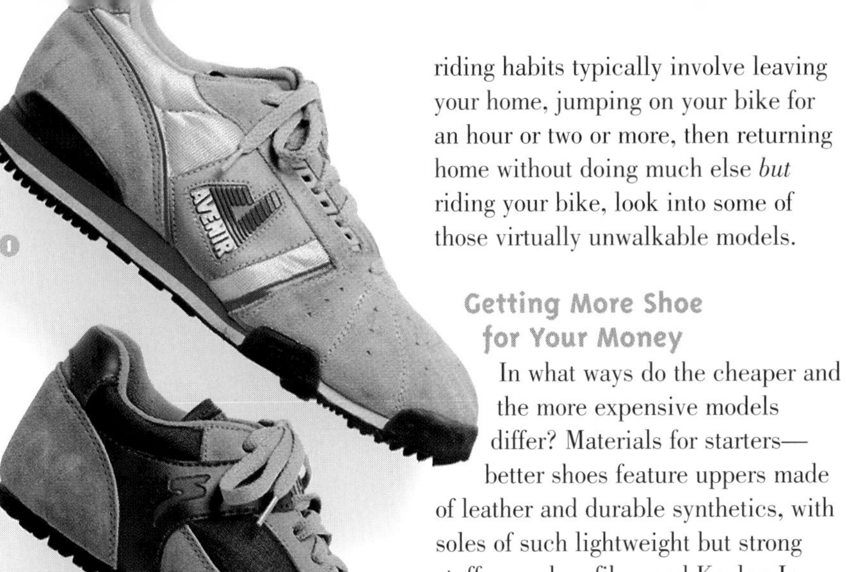

riding habits typically involve leaving your home, jumping on your bike for an hour or two or more, then returning home without doing much else *but* riding your bike, look into some of those virtually unwalkable models.

Getting More Shoe for Your Money

In what ways do the cheaper and the more expensive models differ? Materials for starters—better shoes feature uppers made of leather and durable synthetics, with soles of such lightweight but strong stuff as carbon fiber and Kevlar. In addition, better shoes typically feature more advanced ergonomic contouring and design, in order to push the potential energy-transfer threshold to the max. If you're someone who expects to ride long, hard, and often, every little bit of extra energy helps. But if you're someone who takes riding more casually, you might never notice the slight ergonomic bonus of a more expensive shoe. In that case, don't shell out the big bucks; the less expensive shoes, designed for the more casual cyclist, are also the shoes designed for easier walking and

Touring shoes for road or mountain biking (1) are easy to walk in while still featuring a rigid sole. The extra contour in the soles of more expensive shoes (2) helps in transferring energy to the pedals efficiently. High-performance mountain biking shoes (3) feature greater sole rigidity and contour, with cleats for clipless pedal systems recessed in the sole to facilitate walking. High-performance road shoes (4), with extremely rigid soles and exposed cleats are great for riding but nearly hopeless for walking.

noncycling activities.

Incidentally, a good pair of cycling shoes can last for thousands of miles of riding. The rigid soles help provide structural durability, and because pedaling doesn't (or at least shouldn't) subject a shoe to the kind of bending, twisting, and pounding that might be involved in an activity such as running or hiking, cycling shoes aren't subjected to substantial wear and tear. While an active runner, for example, might go through several pairs of shoes in a year, an active cyclist can count on a good pair of shoes to last for several seasons. So when you're in the store mulling over the extra expenditure for a better shoe, think of it as an investment that will probably pay off in the long term.

SHORTS

Cycling shorts are good for two things: 1) making you more aerodynamic, which is not especially important, and 2) engendering a friendly relationship between your rear end and the bike seat, which is exceedingly important. Saddle sores and skin chafing are the detestable twin banes of all cyclists and are capable of rendering even the mightiest aerobic jock helpless. Eddy Merckx, the legendary Belgian racer, was once forced out of the Tour de France because of boils on his derriere. Cycling shorts are no guarantee against chafing and sores, but riding without cycling shorts for any length of time is a virtual guarantee that something unpleasant *will* happen.

Soft on the Saddle

Just any old pair of Lycra shorts will not do. The key element in a pair of cycling shorts is a sewn-in pad inside the crotch of the shorts, where rear end and saddle meet. This patch used to be made of soft leather chamois. Chamois worked well for three reasons: it was durable, it provided a thin but comfortable cushion between saddle and cyclist, and it minimized abrasiveness where the inner legs and rear end moved against the saddle when the rider was pedaling. But there was a notable drawback: chamois required special care in washing to prevent it from drying out. Without such care, chamois could dry out and end up being more uncomfortable than no chamois at all.

It's still possible to find chamois-lined shorts, but why bother looking? From the wonderful world of fabric technology comes something even better—synthetic chamois. It feels as good as the real thing, can be tossed into a washing machine and come out like new, and, if you're someone who is sensitive about this sort of thing, mountain goats don't have to give up their skin in order to provide the leather to keep your rear end comfy. If you really want a cushy ride, try out a pair of shorts with a gel insert.

Look for a pair of shorts that fit snugly and comfortably over your thighs and quadriceps muscles. The quads are a critical muscular power supply in cycling, so treat them with respect. Well-fitting shorts help to keep the quads warm and also provide at least the comforting illusion of extra support. Another reason to spend a few extra bucks on a better pair of shorts is that the sturdier fabric and better stitching make the shorts less susceptible to the annoying tendency to creep up the leg during the course of a ride. (They will also last longer than less expensive versions, although replacement chamois are available so you can extend the life of your shorts.)

A synthetic fleece pullover is comfortable and warm, sheds moisture well, and is lighter than wool—something to think about if you're packing for a long ride.

Double Up

It is a good idea, by the way, to buy at least two pairs of shorts so that you can be sure to change and wash your shorts regularly. Sweat and bacteria quickly collect in the butt-and-crotch zone. Regular cleaning is more than a matter of obsessive hygiene: it's essential to minimizing the risks of sores and infection. One last preventive measure is to get out of your sweat-soaked shorts as soon as possible after riding.

SHIRTS

The gaudiness of many cycling shirts, advertising-driven though much of it is, actually does have a functional bonus: it makes you visible. If you're somebody who rides often in traffic, visibility is a matter of safety, not just fashion. Nevertheless, it's probably a fair assumption that safety is not deeply considered when most cyclists plunk down between $25 and $70 for shirts screaming a message of bright-colored psychedelia.

Other than safety, a cycling shirt has the functional benefits of being light, aerodynamic, and capable of "wicking" sweat and condensation from the skin. All you need is to see a rider with a loose shirt flapping or ballooning in the breeze to appreciate how much an ill-fitting shirt can act like a parachute, slowing a rider down. It's also nice, especially in a long ride, not to have to deal with the discomfort of a sweaty shirt clinging to your body. That cloying shirt can be a ticket to hypothermia if the air temperature drops or your skin temperature drops when you stop for a rest. Most cycling

GEAR TALK

COOL-WEATHER WEAR

Any coolness in the air tends to become exaggerated by the motion of cycling. When the temperature drops much below 65 degrees F, it's time to slip on leg warmers or long tights. Tights without a padded crotch, and with zippered cuffs, are best, enabling you to slip them easily over your regular cycling shorts and shoes.

Layering is the key to dressing for chillier air; a long-sleeve shirt or sweatshirt (preferably not cotton), a fleece pullover, and a windbreaker are all sensible, light choices that you can don and remove as the temperature dictates. There are special cycling windbreakers that are aerodynamic and often have a rear flap to extend over your rear end. Yet any windbreaker should do fine, as long as it doesn't creep up and is "breathable," allowing the body heat generated by riding to dissipate. Whatever layered outfit you choose, be sure it doesn't constrict your movement or have pronounced seams that might increase the possibility of saddle sores.

Finally, don't forget gloves when the temperature is below 60 degrees. Your hands on the handlebars are exposed to the windchill, and it's impossible to stick them in your pockets for a warm-up while riding. A pair of thin wool or polypropylene gloves is great, because you want something that's warm but not so bulky as to impede shifting, braking, and steering. You'll want some warm socks, too—wool or polypropylene—and if you expect to ride when it's really cold, you might want to invest in cycling "booties" that fit over your cycling shoes.

shirts have pockets on the lower back for carrying food, tools, money, extra water bottles, and so on. But is a cycling shirt really necessary? Not really. For most riding—at least until you start riding hard for long distances—a reasonably snug-fitting T-shirt will do just fine.

Whether gloves are up to protecting this mountain biker's hands is an open question. Nevertheless, they are a valuable addition to the cyclist's wardrobe.

GLOVES

Cycling gloves, with fingers cut off and with padding for the palms, can provide a better grip on the handlebars, especially on hot days when your hands sweat. They are an effective and simple means of shock absorption, lessening the stress and pounding on your hands, wrists, and forearms on a rough ride. Also, gloves protect hands driven by instinct to reach out when falling. That's probably more of a consideration in mountain biking—where falls are more common and the riding surface more abrasive—than it is in road riding.

All of the above are good reasons to wear gloves, but not all cyclists care for them. Gloves can lessen the "feel" for the ground and road surface that many cyclists like for accurate steering and maneuvering of a bike. Poorly fitted gloves can also cut off circulation in the thumbs or fingers.

The only real way to find out if gloves are right for you is trial and error. Try riding *without* gloves for a while first. If you find your hands and wrists getting sore, or if you find your grip slipping on the handlebars, try gloves. (Another cushioning option is padded handlebar tape.) The materials they're made of—some gloves even have gel layers in the palms for extra cushioning—are less important than the fit. Make sure before buying gloves that they fit right when it counts—that is, gripping the handlebars—and not just when you're standing around in a bike shop.

EYEWEAR

Shades add a certain sleekness and ferocity to a cyclist's look, but as windshields and eye protectors, they also serve functional purposes, especially for contact-lens wearers. Shades prevent wind-induced tearing, which can dangerously obscure your vision, and reduce eye- and mind-wearying road glare. They can also deflect insects and foliage, an important consideration for single-track mountain bikers. Shades that provide a large field of vision are best because they're safest; riding with anything that hinders peripheral vision is risky business.

Many models of sport glasses (usually the more expensive models, unfortunately) come with interchangeable lenses of three (or more) tints. Typically, there is a dark tint for sunny days, an amber tint that tends to brighten contrasts on cloudy days, and a clear lens for night riding. If you consider the three-in-one aspect of these glasses, the few extra bucks may be money wisely spent.

Above: A little ingenuity can help when cycling in foul weather. This bicycle messenger in Salt Lake City is wearing a hood under his helmet for added warmth and is using skiing "gaiters" to protect his legs from road slop during a snowstorm. Left: Shades can be functional, as well as look cool, by protecting your eyes from debris and tree branches and by preventing tearing. Different tints can either reduce glare on sunny days or highlight contrasts on gray days.

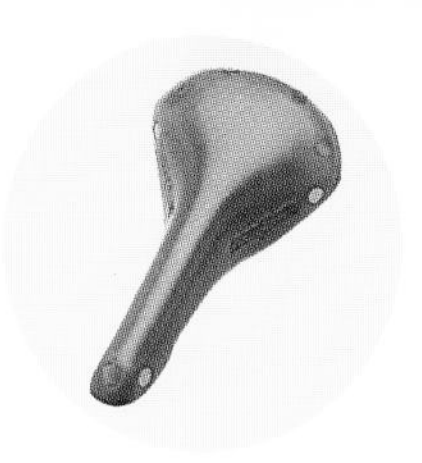

4 READY, SET, RIDE

Don't ever try telling a grown person how to ride a bike. Grown-ups *know* how to ride bikes. Learning to ride is kindergarten stuff, something you do as a kid. What's to learn?

The answer is: plenty. True enough, pretty much everybody is *able* to ride a bike. But riding a bike *effectively* is another story. Beyond the kiddie rudiments of pumping pedals and staying balanced and upright lie an array of subtleties having to do with efficiency, aerodynamics, comfort, safety, and the sheer pleasure that comes from working in smooth sync with the machine.

These subtleties can be taught and learned. Yet most accomplished cyclists end up coming about them through the drudgery and discomfort of thousands of miles of personal trial and error. As good a reason for that as any is that persistent presumption stuck in the national consciousness: everybody knows how to ride a bike. It's like knowing how to walk, speak, or tie shoelaces. What's to learn?

But consider a more practical question: *how* do you learn? Even if you wanted to go back to school in biking basics, where would you go? Zillions of schools teach the proper techniques of tennis, golf, skiing, and a host of other athletic activities. But bicycling schools are a rare breed. The few that do exist are aimed primarily at hard-core racers or people getting started on learning the rela-

When in doubt, it's usually aerobically more efficient to spin a low gear fast rather than try to pound a high gear at lower rpms.

tively nouveau skills of mountain biking.

One reason for this educational vacuum, of course, is that even the sloppiest riding technique still works. Rider pumps pedals, bike goes forward. That's fundamentally unlike, say, golf or tennis, where the effects of sloppy technique are immediately apparent: swing wrong, ball ends up in parking lot.

By improving your riding technique, you'll be able to ride longer, faster, and with less muscle and back fatigue. As trite as it might sound, you'll have more fun. The work of riding that might have been drudgery before can become work that is enjoyable, invigorating, and rewarding. But that transformation will probably come gradually, in almost indiscernible stages over time. Good, efficient riding does not introduce itself through miraculous intervention. It probably won't produce the immediate gratification of, say, a ball struck cleanly down the middle of the fairway.

Instead, learning effective riding comes from repetition, time, and mileage. Some things might feel awkward when you first try them, and you may have to resist mightily an inclination to return to old habits. That said, keep in mind that to ride a bike right, just like performing any athletic activity well, is a process of finding common ground between pedagogy (such as it is in cycling) and personal style. The genius of any good coach in any sport is knowing when to tinker with an athlete's technique and when not to mess. So be your own good coach: learn the basics, experiment with them, adapt them to a personal style that works best for you.

Tim Blumenthal, who heads the International Mountain Biking Association (IMBA), says, "All great road riders are great mountain bikers, and vice versa. The skills are very much the same." In other words, the basics of good, efficient technique work for all kinds of riding: road riding, mountain biking, racing, city riding, and so on. Certainly there are special techniques that apply to specific types of riding, and those will be discussed in Chapter 6. For the time being, concern yourself with the fundamentals.

PROPER POSTURE

Good posture starts with a proper bike fit (see Chapter 2). Before you can develop a comfortable and aerodynamic position, you've got to have a bike that you can, in effect, mold your body to.

Saddle Height

Of course, there are adjustments to make a basically good fit a *really* good fit, the most obvious being an adjustment of saddle height. The height is right when, at the bottom of your pedaling stroke, your leg is *almost* fully extended, but not to the point where your knee locks, you feel strain in your hamstring muscles, or you must roll your butt over slightly in order to reach the bottom of the stroke. Riders differ on how much leg extension they (and their knees) are willing to tolerate, so don't simply set your saddle in one position and consider it a done deal.

Few of us think there is anything to learn about riding a bike beyond what we knew as kids, but there is much to be gained in the enjoyment of cycling from re-examining that assumption.

Once you've got the height right, you will want to fine-tune your saddle adjustment by moving the saddle forward or backward or adding upward or downward tilt. Use signals from your body to guide you: If you feel discomfort in your hamstrings, knees, or Achilles tendons after a fairly long ride (an hour or more), a simple saddle adjustment—up, down, forward, back—could solve the problem. When you make changes to your saddle position, think small. Adjustments of even a quarter of an inch can make a huge difference in your comfort—or discomfort—in the saddle.

Handlebar Position

In addition to adjusting your seat, you may also want to adjust your handlebar height, by raising or lowering the stem. (The stem is the L-shaped element connecting the handlebars to the head tube.) The handlebar level should be slightly below your seat level—as much as four inches lower if you want to ride in a more aerodynamic position.

GEAR TALK

PROPER SIZES OF BIKES

Notice the many differences in posture between a rider fitted perfectly to his bike (right) and the same rider on an ill-fitting machine (left). On a bike that's too small for him, this rider's leg is not fully extended at the bottom of the pedal stroke and his knee is too far forward (the saddle is too low and/or the seat tube is too short), and his upper body is cramped (the top tube is too short).

On his custom fitted bike (right), his leg is nicely extended and his knee is directly over the pedal; his back is at a lower, more comfortable aerodynamic angle; and his arms are in a more extended, comfortable position.

These differences in riding posture may not appear all that great, but after only a few miles—not to mention hours—of riding, they make all the difference in comfort and efficiency.

Bike Too Small

Perfect Fit

Scott Mercer, the 1993 U.S. National Time Trial Champion, drops his chest nearly parallel to the top tube of his bike to achieve a superb aerodynamic position.

The important thing is to have your upper-body mass pitched forward over the pedals, providing more leverage for delivering power to the pedal stroke. If, after fiddling around with the stem height, you still have a hard time settling into a comfortable posture, you might consider buying a new stem. If you have an especially long torso and long arms, for example, a longer stem—the effect of which is to move the handlebars slightly forward—might be just the ticket.

A Straight Back

Another postural element to concentrate on is a straight back. If you want to impress a bunch of bicycle-racing jocks, ride by them with a straight, flat back, flat enough to lay a tea service on. Of course, most riders, especially mountain bikers, rarely position themselves so low on the bike as to get their backs horizontal. Still, a straight back, whether in a fairly upright, angled, or horizontal position, can minimize lower-back and neck strain.

DID YOU KNOW

Moving on your seat backward or forward can significantly improve your cycling performance to take advantage of your particular body type. For example, Chris Carmichael, a coach for the U.S. Cycling Federation, says that cyclists can put strong butt muscles to best use by moving their seat slightly backward and lower. Use caution here, though: Each time you make a shift, move the seat no more than five millimeters in any direction. Overshifting can lead to knee and back strain.

Generally speaking, the straighter the back, the more the skeleton, rather than the musculature, supports your body weight. In addition, a straighter back helps relax the diaphragm, facilitating breathing.

A typical habit of poorly postured riders is to drop their shoulders in an effort to get into a lower, more aerodynamic position—or simply because they're tired. The resulting position bears the look of an angry cat arching its back. To be sure, an arched back can help you take full advantage of shoulder and arm muscles in delivering maximum power to the pedals for short sprints. But a straighter back generally works better for the long haul. So imagine your navel being pulled toward the top tube by some invisible umbilical cord. That will help to keep your back flatter, and get the cat out of your back.

Now just because a cat-less posture might be theoretically better—or work well for other riders—doesn't mean it is right for you. Some people have more natural curvature in the spine than others. For them, trying to maintain a perfectly straight back is a dumb idea. According to Michael Leahy, a chiropractor for the Coors Light racing team, a low aerodynamic posture "puts enormous pressure on the lower back"; an unnatural flattening of the back can deprive parts of the spine of oxygen.

So the best thing you can do is tune into your body's feedback. Sore arms, shoulders, knees, back, and neck are the sorts of problems that can often be corrected by slight postural shifts. Experiment by shifting your rear end forward and backward in the saddle, raising or lowering your shoulders, or bending your elbows. Try gripping the handlebars in various ways; the great advantage of drop bars over straight bars is the number of different hand positions they make possible. Find what works, not necessarily what's right in theory.

Lining Up

Another aspect of good posture is making sure your body—and the parts of your body—are aligned correctly over the bike. The first rule of alignment, whether you're riding with open pedals, toe clips, or cleats, is that the ball of the foot should be directly over the pedal axle. After that, a simple guideline applies: everything, from the hips down, should be lined up on approximately the same vertical plane—the knees, the heels, the balls of the feet. This assures a maximum transfer of force from your stroke to the pedals.

One of the simplest ways for road cyclists to lessen wind resistance is to keep their elbows in, approximately in line with their hands.

Pulling your knees slightly inside that plane is fine if you find that more comfortable. Allowing the knees to drift outside the plane, on the other hand, is woefully inefficient; in a bow-legged position, you short-circuit the power output of your quadriceps, your main power pack. What's more, your bike will tend to wobble from side to side as you pedal. And you are just asking for ligament, knee, and lower back strain. So keep those knees in.

One last alignment matter is the position of your knee, forward or back-

(1) 12:00—heel up, foot light on pedal, preparing to drive down. (2) 2:00—heel drops as foot drives down *and* forward. (3) 5:00—finishing down stroke, beginning to pull back slightly.

ward, relative to the ball of your foot. When your foot is in the three o'clock position on the pedal—in other words, perfectly horizontal—your knee should be directly over the ball of the foot. (You'll probably need the help of a fellow cyclist to determine this accurately.) If the knee is too far forward or back, you are again riding your way into knee problems somewhere down the road. A saddle adjustment or simply a postural adjustment—moving your rear end forward or back in the saddle—should make quick work of correcting a misalignment.

STROKE

Bicycle pedals revolve in a circular, or orbital, pattern. That might sound almost ludicrously obvious. Yet one of the most fundamental flaws of the average rider is to try to enforce an up-and-down motion within that circular pattern: lift straight up, push straight down. But the pedals will continue their orbital pattern no matter how hard you try to force them or will them to do otherwise. So in developing a smooth and efficient stroke, think first of working *with* the round motion of the pedals, not against it. Or to put it another way, get that motion to work for you.

Semantics should get you off to a good start: the word here is *stroke.* It is a word suggesting grace, smoothness, and fluidity. A painter makes strokes with a brush. A stroke is a form of caress. So it is with cycling. Think of stroking the pedals rather than simply pushing them. When you try to force the pedals, by trying to push hard or fast, resistance builds, ultimately to a point of isometric standstill. The best way of avoiding that is to think slow before thinking fast, especially when just starting up, when the pedals put up lots of resistance, or when climbing hills.

Round and Smooth

Start by turning the pedals at a leisurely pace, increasing the pace slowly as your speed increases. Again, concentrate on following the roundness of the pedal movement. If you feel you are losing speed or feel the pedal resistance increasing, don't overreact. Sudden thrusts are the enemies of rhythm and fluidity. Also, those thrusts, especially in mountain biking, can over-torque the rear wheel when you're climbing steep hills. The wheel loses traction and spins uselessly, and next thing you know, you're stopped dead in your tracks. So think round and pick up the pace gradually, with a stroker's mentality. If resistance continues to build, it's time to shift to a lower gear.

Hundreds of ergonomic studies have been conducted on the subject of precisely where, on a pedal's orbit, force is applied most efficiently. And, conversely, where the application of force becomes most inefficient. Not surprisingly, the most power is generated between the two o'clock and five o'clock points in the pedal-stroke orbit. And, not surprisingly, many riders sacrifice stroke fluidity by trying

(4) 6:00—slight pull back, like brushing foot on doormat. (5) 8:00—pull back finished, heel lifting as foot lightens up. (6) 11:00—beginning to lift and drive knee forward to prepare for down stroke.

to maximize that segment of the stroke, even though it represents only about a quarter of the full orbit.

Pressure Points

By improving the circularity of your stroke, you'll start to find new parts of the stroke in which to apply pressure as well as parts where you'll want to relieve pressure almost entirely. At the top of the stroke (the twelve to two o'clock segment) a slight flex of the ankle can change your foot angle, providing the needed leverage to apply pressure. Toward the bottom of the stroke (the five to seven o'clock stretch) you can—especially if your shoes are equipped with cleats—pull back on the pedals. Again, don't force the pedals—work with them, as if brushing your shoe soles lightly on a doormat. Finally, relax and lighten up through the eight to eleven o'clock zone. That provides a millisecond of

BIKE PREP 101: A PRE-RIDE CHECKLIST

Before hitting the road, a quick check to be sure your bike is in good working order can go a long way toward assuring a safe, hassle-free ride. For further details on basic maintenance and repair procedures mentioned here, refer to Chapter 9.

1. Check tires. Look for cuts or loose materials (for example, glass slivers) on the tread. This is especially important for mountain bikers. Stones, glass, and other sharp objects can easily get wedged into those deep treads.
2. Inflate tires. Bike tires are inflated at much higher pressures than car tires, typically between 50 and 100 pounds per square inch (psi). Mountain bikers, seeking extra traction and more shock absorption for loose surfaces, may start with tire pressure of 40 psi or even less. Higher pressure in a smaller tire is harder to maintain; in other words, bike tires lose air pressure much more quickly than car tires. Experienced riders often reinflate their tires before every ride.
3. Check wheels. Make sure the wheels are tightly fastened to the frame and are properly aligned. Give both the front and rear wheels a good tug and shaking to make sure they are secure. If there is any looseness, release the quick-release flange. (All but the least expensive bikes are equipped with quick-release devices to attach wheels to frames. See Chapter 9 for details on how to adjust the quick-release device.) Give it a quick, tightening twist (or two), then resecure the wheel. Make sure the wheels are aligned straight between the frame

recuperation for your muscles with each stroke. It also lessens the work-load of your opposite foot, which at that point is in its downward thrust.

CADENCE

"Cadence" or "turnover" are cycling terms for the rate (per minute) of pedaling revolutions. (A revolution, by the way, means a full revolution of one pedal. A good way to count revolutions is to chalk one up each time the left or right foot reaches the bottom of the stroke.) Some ergonometric studies have shown that maximum cycling power is generated in the 50 to 60 revolutions-per-minute (rpm) range. Yet experienced riders typically say that 70 to 80 rpm feels about right. When subjected to ergonometric tests, Lance Armstrong, the 1993 world professional road racing champion, proved most effective pedaling in the low 70s.

---

stays and the brake pads.

❹ Check brakes. Make sure the brakes are centered and the pads aligned over the rims, not the tires. Make sure cable tension is set right for accurate braking and that there is no slack in the cable.

❺ Clean and lube the chain. Quickly run a cloth with a degreasing solvent over the chain, then apply, sparingly, a thin layer of lubricant. This is not essential before every ride, but keeping your chain clean will ensure a smooth-working drivetrain.

❻ Bring water and food. Water or other fluids are essential for any ride of half an hour or more, especially in warm weather. Dehydration, announcing itself in the form of dizziness, headaches, muscle weakness, and cramps, can not only be debilitating but downright dangerous. It's better to take too much water than too little, because water you don't drink can always be used to squirt over your head or legs as a coolant. For any ride of two hours or more, you'll need easy-to-eat food (fruit, energy bars, or the like) to replenish your body's fuel supply.

❼ Bring repair gear. An extra inner tube (or tire), a pump (or compressed-air cartridges), tire irons, and a patch kit are most important. A small adjustable wrench and a set of hex (or Allen) wrenches are useful for making brake, derailleur, and seat adjustments. A screwdriver may come in handy.

❽ Look for anything obviously wrong. Loose screw, dangling cable, broken spoke, a crack in the frame—if it's broke and reparable, fix it. If you don't have the tools or the know-how, get your bike to a shop for immediate service—just don't *ride* it!

Drive train comparison: Two chain rings on a road bike (top) make for less shifting range in the lowest gears for generally flatter riding terrain. Notice that the cogset cluster in the rear is also smaller, providing a narrower range. The mountain bike (bottom) has a third, smaller chain ring for the low gears needed for climbing steep grades. Three chain rings x 8 cogwheels = 24 gears, the maximum for mountain bikes.

Greg LeMond, the only American to win the Tour de France (three times, in fact), prefers a higher cadence of around 90 rpm. So who is right, Greg, Lance, or the lab jocks?

The answer is all of them, in their individual ways. The lab tests indicate an optimal cadence for delivery of power to the pedals, but not necessarily power delivered over the long haul. The racing jocks seek a cadence that allows for an optimal combination of power and cardiovascular endurance. Armstrong's and LeMond's preferred cadences differ simply because their physical makeups differ. Similarly, the cadence you settle on will be a factor both of your cardiovascular condition, the smoothness of your stroke, and your own unique physiology. You might find that 70 rpm feels sluggish, while you might also find it a struggle to maintain a smooth stroke at 90 rpm. But ultimately what you should be shooting for is a comfortable cadence that falls within that range.

Finding Your Rhythm

A smooth stroke is certainly more important than a few rpm, plus or minus, in your cadence. A mechanically inefficient stroke makes for more work, overtaxing your muscles and cardiovascular system just as an uncomfortable cadence can. So for starters, settle in at a relatively slow cadence—around 60 rpm—and concentrate on rounding out your stroke.

When you've got the hang of stroking at that cadence, pick up the pace, gradually working your way up toward 90 rpm. You should learn to become comfortable stroking smoothly at up to 100 rpm, at least for short stretches, even if your ideal cadence is quite a bit lower.

Keep in mind that the cadence of the average cyclist is typically lower than an optimal rate, especially when climbing hills. But when your cadence is *too* low, your muscles work harder, and lactic acid fills the muscles. You needn't know what lactic acid is to recognize its painful, leaden presence in your muscles. Also, the increased pedal resistance of lower cadences can lead to knee strain or injury.

Getting up to Speed

One simple tactic for increasing your cadence is to ride in especially low gears. You might at first feel like you're spinning wildly, with your feet desperately chasing the pedals through their orbits. But stick with it; the lesser resistance in the pedals at lower gears should make it fairly easy to pick up your cadence without tiring your leg muscles. You might find yourself breathing harder than you're used to, since you are probably shifting your cardiovascular system into a new gear. That's a good sign; now concentrate on synchronizing your breathing with your pedal strokes—say, two strokes and exhale, two strokes and exhale. Whatever works for you. Pretty soon your breathing, heartbeat, and stroke cadence will be on the same metronomic pace, ushering in a new, aerobic synchronization in your riding.

SHIFTING GEARS

A theoretical ideal to shoot for would be to ride within the same cadence

GEAR TALK

CYCLING COMPUTERS

Cycling computers, starting at around $25, have been a terrific addition over the last decade to cycling gadgetry. No, they aren't devices for tapping into the Internet or playing CD-ROM games. They simply provide some very useful information: how fast you're riding, how far you've ridden, your average speed, the rate of your cadence, and so on. Having that kind of direct feedback available in a display on your handlebars can help in your search for optimal riding efficiency and pleasure. Using speed and cadence functions, for example, you can determine when you're pushing too hard and when you're not pushing hard enough. Mostly it's just fun to know how fast and far you've gone.

The mountain-bike cogset (left) has more cogs (8) and more teeth per cog (32 on the largest cog) than the road-bike cogset (right) which has 7 cogs, with only 21 teeth on the largest cog. In short, more cog teeth mean more lower gears for easier climbing up steep slopes.

range throughout a ride. That would be easy if the world were perfectly flat. There would be no need for elaborate gear-shifting systems. And in fact, track racers, who deal only with flat surfaces, have bikes with only one gear.

Because the world isn't flat, different gears allow you to stay within a cadence range regardless of the ups

TECHNIQUE TIP

DESPERATELY SEEKING SMOOTHNESS

Still having a hard time getting a feel for that smooth, round stroke? Two tips might help.

1. "Follow the leader." Find a flat spot or a gentle downhill, and pedal up to a fairly high speed. Then stop applying pedal pressure; simply allow your feet to follow the pedals through several rotations. Concentrate on feeling where the pedals are at every point of the rotation, not necessarily where your walking instincts want to push them. Then gradually increase your foot pressure again, still following the lead of the pedals.
2. "The one-foot wonder." This will work only if you have toe clips or cleats. Simply try pedaling with one foot only. That will force you to use all of the pedal stroke. To keep the pedal turning, you'll find you have to initiate your push early, at the twelve o'clock position, and pull at the bottom of the stroke, starting at about the five o'clock position.

and downs encountered on a ride. Gear tables usually measure front and back gear combinations in inches, referring to the number of inches a bike travels forward in one full pedal revolution. For example, the combination of a 52-tooth chain ring in front and a 14-tooth cog in back propels the bike forward 100.3 inches. That's a pretty high gear, about as high as you'll find on an average bike. Something like a 40 x 17 gear, a good cruising gear for the average rider on a flat, paved surface, propels the bike 63.5 inches. A mountain biker climbing a hill with a gradient exceeding 15 percent might go with a gear smaller than 30 inches.

Anticipate the need to down shift by assessing terrain changes well ahead of you. Waiting too late to drop to a lower gear on a steep hill can throw off your pace or even make you stall out.

A gear table might help you visualize exactly what a particular gear does for you and how different gear combinations compare. But gearing is really a matter of feel rather than arithmetic. As you feel changes in pedal resistance, plus or minus, you should shift accordingly, ideally not missing a beat in your cadence.

Most riders, however, underutilize

the array of gears on their bikes. One reason, of course, is that the act of shifting is often awkward. Shifting gears usually involves at least some change of hand position, even if it is just a matter of flicking the thumb or forefinger to work handlebar-mounted shifters. Shifting can cause a slight hiccup in the flow of the chain over the gear rings. With that comes a momentary change in cadence, a momentary lapse in concentration on the road, a slight wobble, all of which can affect a cyclist's sense of balance and control. Too often a cyclist would rather stay in an inefficient gear than sacrifice the feeling of control.

The position of gear-shifting levers on most mountain bikes—within thumb's reach of the grips—eases that concern considerably. In mountain biking, where rough terrain can play havoc with control and balance, being able to shift gears without moving your hands from the grips is essential. A relatively new design that is becoming popular on road bikes with drop bars is the incorporation of shift levers in the brake levers, also making shifting easier without moving the hands much.

Don't Be Shiftless

Regardless of where your shift levers are, use them! Practice shifting in

TECHNIQUE TIP

LOOKING BACK

An essential part of safe riding is knowing what's happening behind you. Turning to look back is easy enough, but in doing so riders often swerve—slightly or dramatically—in the direction they're turning. In traffic, that can be extremely dangerous. You need to develop an ability to look back and steer a straight course simultaneously.

The main trick is to minimize movement of your torso. Shifting your torso shifts your center of balance, hence causing the bike to swerve. To prepare for looking back, start by slowing down. Lift up on the handlebars if you are riding in a low position. Then turn your head by using as little shoulder turn as possible. Tucking your chin downward toward your collarbone, rather than just turning your head on a horizontal plane, is one way to lessen your shoulder turn.

If you need a really broad view of what's up behind you, stop pedaling, sit up on the bike, and turn your shoulders without turning your hips. That shoulder turn may tend to pull the bike in the direction of the turn; to counterbalance that pull, extending the opposite knee outward may help. Practice these maneuvers when not in traffic so that you are comfortable pulling them off when you really need them.

Getting out of the saddle for quick bursts can help in sprinting or short hill climbs. Notice that the racer in blue is using his large chain ring, while the racer in red is using his small chain ring. That's probably why the blue racer is farther out of his saddle—he needs extra oomph to drive a higher gear.

areas where you feel safe and comfortable—in a flat area away from traffic. Get the feel not only for shifting smoothly but for the effect it has on your cadence. Smooth, timely shifting is most important for riding uphill. As a general rule for going uphill—and as an absolute rule before facing a sudden steep climb while mountain biking—shift gears *before* shifting is necessary. On steep uphills, you can stall out remarkably quickly if in too high a gear. At that point, getting back on the bike and restarted on a steep incline can be difficult. Don't be too concerned about over-shifting (shifting into too small a gear) in this situation. You'll just end up spinning a little

TECHNIQUE TIP

SHIFT SPIN SHIFT

Juli Furtado, two-time world and four-time national mountain biking champion, is no different than any other sensible cyclist—she doesn't like to work any harder than she has to when climbing a steep hill. "I like to sit down and spin (in a low gear) as much as possible," says Furtado. "I try to save energy by shifting on the seat, backwards and forwards. That way I use all of my muscles—buttocks, quads, calves—rather than tiring out one set of muscles."

faster—something you might want to be doing anyway.

BRAKING

Braking is much less about stopping than it is about speed control. As such it comes into play much more in mountain biking on steep, single-track trails than it does in road riding.

Shift your weight far back, be ready to brake at all times, and be alert to the terrain ahead of you—key elements to descending successfully on off-road terrain.

Speeds are changing constantly due to constantly changing terrain. Nevertheless, on road or off, the basic principle of braking is the same: apply pressure gradually. Bike brakes work much more smoothly and effectively when pressure between the brake pad and the wheel rim is allowed to build gradually.

For that reason, braking is much more effective when you anticipate, rather than simply react, to a need to slow down. The descending mountain biker is virtually absorbed with this thought—looking ahead and trying to anticipate a call to apply the brakes.

TECHNIQUE TIP

BRAKE DANCING

Shortly after beginning a ride, play with your brakes a little to make sure they're in good working order. "Feather" them lightly and rhythmically to be sure the grip is sure and even. Do this again at the beginning of a long descent; you don't want to hit the brakes, especially when traveling in excess of 30 mph on a long downhill, only to discover that they're out of order. Also repeat the process periodically if you're riding in the rain or on wet surfaces. And don't be misled by squeaks or squeals. Bike brakes often sound off noisily while still functioning properly.

The mountain biker who fails to anticipate and applies the brakes suddenly usually ends up performing the dreaded "end-o," as in end-over. The bike stops but the mountain biker doesn't, flying over the handlebars.

Take It Easy

Riding on paved roads usually doesn't call for such uninterrupted vigilance, although you should always use extra caution on any road you've never ridden before. Still, you should be looking ahead for corners, intersections, traffic, hills, and so on, to give yourself plenty of time to apply gradual, rather than sudden, brake pressure. That will also give you time to set your body in a centered and balanced position that won't be thrown out of whack when you do apply the brakes. If you brake properly, your body and your bike should decelerate at the same speed. If your body mass shifts forward on the bike—the end-o being the extreme example—you're either off-balance or hitting the brakes too hard.

When you reach the top of a long hill, smile and enjoy the feeling of a job well done.

TECHNIQUE TIP

LET MOMENTUM BE YOUR FRIEND

Do you find yourself getting bounced around when the road gets rough? "If you have trouble getting over or through rough surfaces, slowing down might not be the answer," says Bill Strickland, associate editor of *Bicycling* magazine. Instead, says Strickland, speeding up a little can go a long way in helping smooth out the ride. That doesn't mean launching into an all-out sprint mode; just try to maintain your forward momentum to get your wheels rolling more smoothly over the rough spots.

Apply pressure equally to both brake levers; while the front brake provides most of the braking force, equal pressure assures that you'll slow down in a straight direction, rather than skidding or swerving. The exception here is mountain biking on very steep descents, where applying more braking action with the rear brake can provide more stability.

RELAX!

If you feel like you're working too hard, you probably are. Tension has a way of building up in the body the more tired you get, and many riders have an almost perverse tendency to fight tension rather than relieve it. Hunched over, with a vise-like grip on the handlebars, face in a contorted grimace—the tense, tired rider appears more intent on *willing* a bike forward than riding it. His or her destiny is anaerobic, isometric, muscle-weary, back-aching hell.

One of the great things about cycling as exercise is the opportunity it affords to relax completely, by coasting, in the middle of a ride. (Imagine trying to do so while running—you'd come to a stop.) Stop pedaling for a while, or stand up on the pedals to stretch your back, legs, and arms. It is nothing less than miraculous how far the body can go in restoring itself in even a few seconds of complete relaxation.

Tension Zones

Different people store tension in different places. Popular tension zones for cyclists are the back, hands, forearms, jaw, neck, and feet. After you've been riding a few miles, take a moment to coast and ascertain where tension is building. Make a conscious effort to send a message to those parts of the body: lighten up. Uncurl your toes. Loosen your grip on the handlebars. Drop your shoulders. Wipe the grimace off your face and smile. As you become more confident and your riding becomes smoother, work on delivering these same relaxation messages while pedaling.

5 SMART CYCLING

It is the lamentable predicament of cyclists in America to have long been relegated to second-class citizenship among travelers. Face the facts: on the vast majority of the roads and trails you might want to ride, cyclists are not considered primary users. Most roads are built for automotive traffic. Most trails were created with hikers or horseback riders in mind. Sidewalks are for pedestrians.

In the total American road-and-trail mix, the number of paths, trails, and lanes built for bicycles represents a paltry percentage. As a result, you, as a cyclist, are usually regarded as an interloper, fairly or unfairly, almost anywhere you ride. Your right there might well be inalienable and indisputable, but others on the road or trail are apt to be less than obliging in recognizing that right.

Fighting for Respect

Many avid cyclists, both road riders and mountain bikers, react to this second-class-citizen status with fervent activism—to good and sometimes not-so-good effect. On the positive side, organizations such as Transportation Alternatives in New York City have made significant headway in promoting urban bike use and encouraging local governments to make room for cyclists on their byways. Portland (Oregon), Seattle, and Washington, D.C., have been

DID YOU KNOW

In the 1890s, cyclists were the most vocal proponents of upgrading city streets and country highways. Cyclists were the first road users to issue regular reports on road conditions. (from *A Social History of the Bicycle,* by Robert A. Smith)

leaders of the pack in developing bike-friendly urban environments.

On the off-road scene, the International Mountain Biking Association and its affiliated regional organizations have led the way in promoting conscientious and courteous mountain biking. Among IMBA's notable successes has been encouraging the Sierra Club, the environmental organization, to soften its once hard line on mountain biking. Such efforts have gone far in defusing a confrontational attitude between trail users—those on bikes and those on foot in particular—and to open more trails to riding.

However, not all mountain bikers have been as diplomatic, farsighted, or politically savvy. There remain many mountain bikers who believe that the trail-use rights of cyclists should match those of hikers and horseback riders. Their feeling is that, in being disallowed from many trails, they are being discriminated against.

In many cases, they are. Yet mountain bikers, as the new kids on the trail-use block, bear the extra obligation of having to prove their worthiness to land managers and other trail users. By being overly aggressive in asserting their presumed trail rights, a small number of renegade riders have only served to galvanize the ire of those who disapprove of

When there is a paved shoulder, stay toward the inside of it; the outer edges of shoulders are usually strewn with gravel and sharp debris that cause punctures. At the same time, be prepared for the buffeting back drafts of trucks.

mountain biking.

When trail-use squabbles arise, mountain bikers, like it or not, almost always get dealt the short end of the stick by land managers in national parks, national forests, state parks, and recreation areas. Lingering uncertainties about the safety and environmental implications of mountain-bike use haven't helped the cause of riders. So at the slightest whiff of acrimony or confrontation, land managers as often as not have gone with the quick, cut-and-dried solution: ban bikes from trails.

When there is no shoulder, stay far to the right and ride single-file. If the rider in the rear moved two feet to his right, he'd be less likely to impede traffic and he'd have less work to do by "drafting" behind the rider in front of him.

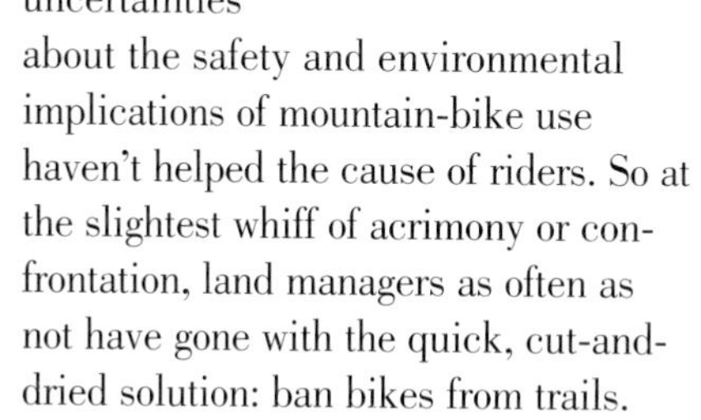

A Spirit of Sharing

The newness of mountain biking has made the incendiary trail-use debate cycling's issue of the moment. But in the overall picture of bike use in America, it's old hat, linked to that fundamental premise: cyclists are secondary users of roads and trails created for the use of other travelers.

There is a simple way to deal with that fact: accept it and be willing to share the road (or trail). It is a spirit of sharing—a willingness to acknowledge other trail users—that has empowered IMBA to make inroads with the hiking-oriented Sierra Club and with the U.S. Forest Service on behalf of mountain bikers. But a spirit of sharing should not be considered simply a device used by cycling organizations as bargaining leverage; it is an attitude that all cyclists need to adopt—for their own safety, if for no better reason.

SAFE CYCLING

Sharing means recognizing the existence and right of passage of other travelers, wherever you ride, and responding accordingly. It means being guided by two of the most fundamental principles of smart, responsible cycling—safety and sensitivity, both to others and to the environment.

The Letter of the Law

Riding safely is a matter of staying in control of your bike and obeying the rules of the road. The rules to be outlined here (as well as those in the IMBA "Rules of the Trail" on page 95) are based on common sense and courtesy, not necessarily on law or local ordinance. This doesn't, however, absolve you of the obligation to know and obey the laws or ordinances in any particular area. You might want to contact a local or state department of transportation on cycling ordinances, just to cover your bases.

On the road, cyclists are expected to abide by regular traffic laws—stopping at lights and stop signs, yielding to traffic when required, staying within speed limits, and so on. There are times, of course, when strict adherence to the law is pretty silly—coming to a

PLANNING FOR BICYCLE USE

The Intermodal Surface Transportation Efficiency Act of 1991 (ISTEA) is such a mouthful that most people refer to it as "ice tea." Apart from being nearly impossible to say in one breath, ISTEA is a piece of legislation unknown to most Americans. This is unfortunate, because bicyclists especially can benefit from ISTEA's provisions.

The purpose of ISTEA is to "develop a National Intermodal Transportation System that is economically efficient and environmentally sound, provides the foundation for the Nation to compete in the global economy, and will move people and goods in an energy efficient manner." Worthy goals, but what does this mean for cyclists? Among other things, it means funding for the construction of paved and pebble-surface bicycle and multiuse trails, for signage of designated bike routes, and for bicycle lockers and racks.

ISTEA calls for public participation at the local level, which means you can probably plug your energies into those of an existing local bicycle organization. National groups like the Bicycle Federation of America, the League of American Bicyclists, and the Rails-to-Trails Conservancy are all actively involved with securing ISTEA funds for bicycle use. (Check the resources for ways to contact these organizations.) Assorted environmental groups, the National Trust for Historic Preservation, and the Surface Transportation Policy Project are other groups working to improve conditions for cyclists and pedestrians. Even your state department of transportation will have information on bicycle use and planning—so find out what's going on in your area!

STPP can be reached at 1400 Sixteenth Street, N.W., Suite 300, Washington, D.C. 20036; 202-939-3470.

The key to smart cycling: Keep your eyes focused on the road ahead, especially on busy streets.

complete, put-your-foot-down stop at a rural intersection, for example. While you might be expected to use hand signals to indicate all turns, there are times when removing a hand from the handlebars would be unsafe. Be guided by safety and common sense as well as the law.

Stick to the Open Road or Trail

The first rule of safe cycling is to ride only where you're allowed to ride. If you see a sign with a cyclist slashed by a red line, its meaning should be obvious. On roads, cyclists are often prohibited in places they wouldn't want to ride anyway—interstate highways and urban expressways, for example.

Mountain bikers, on the other hand, are often prohibited from prime riding terrain. Again, it is up to you to know where you're allowed to ride and where you aren't. Trail closures should be indicated at trailheads and crossings, but the signage is often easy to miss. You should stop at all trailheads and crossings, just to be sure cyclists are allowed to proceed. The best policy is: when in doubt, don't.

Be Aware of the World

The second rule is more vague: be keenly aware of the world around you as you ride. Be aware of the nature of the surface you're riding—rough, smooth, wet, dry, paved, loose—and how that affects your control of your bike. The distance required to brake to a full stop on gravel or on wet pavement, for example, is typically several times the braking distance for hard, dry surfaces.

Not all cyclists agree that hand signals to indicate turns or stops are a good idea. Letting motorists know your intentions might seem sensible, yet taking one hand off your handlebars (and brake lever) while in traffic is often a bad idea. And you can't assume all motorists recognize hand signals. Your best bet is to react to traffic movements—letting cars pass and making direction changes only when you're sure the coast is clear.

DID YOU KNOW

Stephen Breyer, appointed to the Supreme Court in 1994, commutes to work by bike. Despite a serious crash in 1993 that put him in the hospital with broken ribs and a punctured lung, Breyer is back in the saddle of his unfashionable old three-speed, doing daily rides from his Washington home to the court and back.

Know where your fellow riders are in relation to you. Anticipate terrain changes and intersections. Know when vehicles or other trail users are approaching you from any direction. One bit of unfortunate news here: riding with a disc or tape player and earphones robs you of a key sense—hearing—needed to be a safe, aware rider. It's not a smart idea, and in parts of the country it is illegal.

Stay Straight

The third rule of safe cycling is to steer a straight, predictable course. Weaving around is a hazard to yourself, others you're riding with, and other road or trail users. To be sure,

GEAR TALK

LIGHTS AND REFLECTORS

If you ride at night or in dim light, reflectors *and* lights are essential. That's especially true if you use your bike for commuting; you never know when you might get stuck at the office after hours and have to ride home unexpectedly at night.

Many bikes come equipped with reflectors on the spokes. While no reflector is a bad reflector, these are probably the least useful, reflecting light only when crossing a motorist's path. By the time the motorist picks up the reflection, it's often too late to react. More important are reflectors or, even better, pulsing lights projecting forward and backward. Those pulsing lights aren't especially expensive ($12 and up). You can get taillights to mount on your seatpost, rear stays, and even your helmet. Make sure before you head off in the dark that the lights are clear of mud and debris.

Headlights—most are handlebar-mounted, but a few can be mounted on your helmet—are a great idea, at least to indicate your presence to oncoming traffic. But few cast enough light to illuminate much of the road ahead. Headlights do not do away with the most important rule of night riding: *slow down.* Riding fast at night is lunacy.

Incidentally, makers of bicycle wear have been admirably conscientious about jumping on the safety wagon by incorporating reflective strips on the backs of shoes, helmets, clothing, and bike bags. Another way to increase your visibility is to add reflective tape in strategic places like your fenders, seat stays, and racks. Most bicycle and sporting goods stores also sell reflectorized leg bands and "slow-moving vehicle" triangles that can further increase your visibility, as will wearing light-colored clothing.

Stay alert to your surroundings, stay to the right, and steer a straight, predictable course.

you'll at times need to change course to avoid obstacles—potholes, rocks, branches, stumps, broken glass. But by focusing down the road or trail, you should be able to make those course deviations without veering suddenly. Before changing course, let riders behind you know what's happening. Alert them to the presence of some obstruction or nasty stretch of pavement ahead.

Incidentally, it should go without saying yet . . . *always* ride in the direction of traffic. The once-promoted idea of riding against traffic—presumably to allow converging drivers and riders to see one another coming—is sheer lunacy. Just do the math: the speed differential of a car going 40 mph overtaking a cyclist going 15 mph is 25 mph; the differential of car and cyclist converging at those speeds is 55 mph. The potential force of impact is more than doubled, while the reaction time for both rider and driver is dramatically reduced. By staying to the right, steering a straight course, and being aware of circumstances around you, you're much safer going in the direction of traffic.

Sensitive Cycling

Whether riding on a busy highway, a designated recreational path, or a secluded mountain trail, it is essential to be alert to at least the *possibility* of encountering other road or trail users. At times, such encounters might be so frequent as to be a frustration or an annoyance, especially in or close to heavily populated areas. Heavy, horn-honking traffic, bands of Boy Scouts out for a hike, groups of horseback riders, swarms of in-line skaters or runners, even swarms of other cyclists do not make for pleasant riding. Yet steering clear of such problem situations is often easier than you might think. As obvious as it sounds, you can simply do your riding elsewhere. The versatility of bikes, after all, enables them to go many places. Or make an effort to ride in heavily used areas only during off-peak hours.

. . . On the Road

Stick to the far right and ride on the shoulder if there's one that's ridable. To be sure, shoulders are often strewn with debris and gravel, or are composed of soft dirt rather than pavement, and can be hazardous. So your rule of thumb should be to stay as far to the right as is safely possible. Don't overdo it; give yourself some leeway in

GEAR TALK

REAR-VIEW MIRRORS

Do you need a rearview mirror? Legally, no, but for safety reasons it's an accessory you might consider. A rearview mirror can either be mounted on your handlebars or, if it's a mirror resembling the ones dentists use when prying into your mouth, on your helmet. Neither is necessarily better than the other; it's your choice to determine which design you feel more comfortable with.

As sensible a device as a rearview mirror might seem, it still comes with caveats. For starters, any mirror must be mounted properly, providing a clear view to your left rear, whence most passing traffic is coming. You'll need to readjust often, since the jolts of the road can throw proper adjustment out of whack. When you look into your mirror, make an effort to minimize your head movements. Head movements lead to body movements, meaning the *bike* tends to move, diverting you from steering straight.

Finally, a rearview mirror is no substitute for being able to turn your head and look back over your shoulder safely (see Technique Tip, page 76). Mirrors provide only a limited field of vision and, especially on bumpy roads, not always a reliable one. Even if you have a mirror, practice and become comfortable with looking behind you.

Do nature a favor: Stick to the trail when riding, especially in desert, semi-arid, and tundra environments, where plants have a hard enough time growing as it is.

case you deviate slightly to your right or are discombobulated by the air turbulence of passing traffic. If there still isn't enough room to allow other traffic to pass safely, find another road to ride.

Be aware of traffic coming up behind you and prepare yourself for it. Buffeting back drafts from fast-moving trucks can be particularly disconcerting. Don't tense up, but *do* brace yourself, again concentrating on maintaining a straight course. All cars and trucks might not heckle you with their horns the minute they see you, but be ready for it; you don't want to find yourself jumping out of the saddle at the sound of a horn blast.

Never ride more than two abreast. Anything else is both dangerous and disruptive to traffic. Cars and trucks are bigger and more powerful than cyclists and many drivers, however wrong-minded, don't recognize the right of cyclists to use the road. No reason to get them hot and bothered by taking up any more of the road than you have to. Single-file riding is even better (if less sociable) and in most cases essential on roads without shoulders, especially around sharp curves where sight lines are obscured.

. . . On the Trail

IMBA's rule on single-track trails is simple: yield to others. As likely as not, "others" means people on foot. Overly aggressive mountain bikers—"hammerheads," as they're sometimes called—may view yielding as a form of surrender. What nonsense! If a trail is so heavily used by hikers that you'd be off your bike yielding the trail much of the time, why would you want to be on that trail in the first place? On the other hand, if you find yourself yielding to hikers every couple of miles—perhaps even less—what's the big dif? Yielding is safe and tactful and goes far toward mollifying the potentially contentious relationship between hikers and riders.

Other likely "others" are horseback riders. Yielding in the case of an encounter with horses should be a no-brainer. For starters, horses, like cars,

Use good judgment: If riding on a particular trail will contribute to severe erosion, do your riding elsewhere and give the trail a chance to recover.

When a sign indicates no cycling, it means no cycling, even if the trail is open to hikers or horseback riders.

are considerably bigger than cyclists. Unlike cars, horses have potentially volatile temperaments. Riding a fast-moving bike in the tight quarters of a backcountry trail is a great way to spook a horse into rearing or bolting.

Yielding, by the way, doesn't always require that you must dismount, move off the trail, and kowtow to others as they pass by. Many trails are wide enough to allow trail users to pass one another safely. Yielding *does* mean slowing way down and assuring a wide enough avenue for others to pass without feeling confronted or alarmed. If there is any question whatsoever, stop and move over.

Sensitivity to the Environment

Until interest in mountain biking began booming in the 1980s, the environmental sensitivity of cycling—except when it came to such obvious matters as littering—was never much of an issue. Roads, after all, were built for gas-burning vehicles, and cycling was universally regarded as environmentally friendly. Better to fill the roadways with environmentally benign cyclists than with exhaust-spewing motorists.

Environmental issues regarding mountain biking are far more complex and still not well understood. Mountain biking hasn't been around long enough for environmentalists to determine accurately its damage potential compared with, say, hiking or horseback riding. As a result, mountain bikers are left to be guided by their own environmental presumptions and by a handful of localized, inconclusive test studies and not always by good sense.

Sticking to back roads—as here in the San Juan Mountains of southern Colorado—doesn't mean you have to miss out on the beauty of the backcountry.

TRAIL EROSION. A few reports suggesting that mountain bikes cause no more trail erosion than hikers or horses have emboldened some riders to believe that they're now at liberty to proceed full speed ahead. Yet the erosion data regarding mountain biking remains woefully incomplete. And just because mountain bikers might be in the same league as hikers or horseback riders in causing trail erosion shouldn't be regarded as a license to blast away. Erosion, whether caused by boots, hooves, or bike tires, is still erosion.

Sitting squarely on his bike, with his helmet on, fingers at the brake levers, eyes alert to the trail ahead, this young mountain biker has put all the elements of safe riding together.

Tim Blumenthal, IMBA's executive director, also raises concerns about the "testosterone poisoning of young, aggressive thrill-seekers" who have come to mountain biking "lacking a backcountry ethic." Athletic challenge, rather than wilderness appreciation, is their main objective, often to the detriment of delicate environments. "They represent a smaller and smaller percentage of all mountain bikers," says Blumenthal, but, with mountain biking's growth, "they are a smaller percentage of a larger number."

Furthermore, environmental sensitivity is not something that mountain biking's image crafters have done much to promote. To the contrary, magazine and advertising photographs are more inclined to romanticize the sport at the expense of a prudent respect for the environment. All too often, riders are shown in some inspiring setting—for example, meandering across a tundra meadow of wildflowers—or hammering some gnarly, muddy trail. Looks cool, but what kind of environmental message is being delivered?

LIGHT RIDING. A few years ago, the U.S. Forest Service and the Bureau of Land Management initiated a program called "Tread Lightly," to "urge safe, environmentally responsible use of public and private lands." The program was designed primarily with motorized off-road vehicles in mind, but mountain bikes were considered to belong under the program umbrella.

To be lumped together with noisy, exhaust-emitting machinery is just the sort of thing that, justifiably, can rile dedicated mountain bikers. Nevertheless, some of the Tread Lightly recommendations are well worth heeding, notably: comply with all signs and barriers; ask an owner's permission to cross private property; and *most important* (emphasis added) avoid streams, lake shores, meadows, and muddy roads and trails. Sure, there might be times when you can or must cross streams and meadows when in the backcountry, or when you find muddy going unavoidable. But if you take the program's heading—Tread Lightly—as a guiding principle, you'll probably do all right in those situations.

WILDLIFE AWARENESS. If the erosive impact of mountain biking is still not well understood, the impact on wildlife remains even more of a muddle. A few things *are* known, notably that the speed at which mountain bikers travel can be problematic in encountering wildlife. Park rangers in the Canadian Rockies, for example, have concluded that, in a couple of cases, bear maulings of mountain bikers were most likely attributable to riders unknowingly zipping through the scent line between mother and cubs. Crossing that scent line is a mother bear's call to arms. Speed is only part of the problem; riders taking on technically demanding terrain usually, by necessity, are concentrating on the trail, rather than the world around them. That only increases the chances of an abrupt, unexpected, and possibly unpleasant wildlife encounter.

The National Audubon Society, in *Travel Ethic for Environmentally Responsible Travel,* an eco-tourism manual, provides a few commonsense guidelines for dealing with wildlife that mountain bikers would do well to adopt. "Never . . . surround an animal

RULES OF THE TRAIL

The following are the International Mountain Biking Association's guidelines for responsible "soft" use of single-track trails:

1. Ride on open trails only
2. Leave no trace
3. Control your bike
4. Always yield trail
5. Never spook animals
6. Plan ahead

or group of animals," "never get between animal parents and their young," and "animals (should) not be harassed or approached too closely" are among the key principles advocated by the society. The society also includes special caution about disturbing nesting and breeding cycles.

DO NOT DISTURB. To minimize the chances of disturbing wildlife, you can do two things. The first is to check with local forest or park rangers or game wardens before entering a particular area, especially if you're embarking on a multi-day outing. Ask about the presence of wildlife—especially bears—and about migratory patterns, foraging habits, and breeding cycles. Ask about places that should be avoided or where you should be particularly sensitive to the possible presence of wildlife.

The second thing is simply to heighten your awareness of the world around you, especially as you ride deeper and deeper into the backcountry. Look as far down the trail as is safely possible, not simply at the ground immediately in front of you. Make an extra effort to keep your speed down on single-track trails on which your peripheral vision is limited by trees and tall grasses.

As more becomes understood about the environmental impact of mountain biking, guidelines and regulations on backcountry usage are drawn up and applied. Like it or not, you must stick to the rules, which may vary considerably from one area to the next. But also, consider the following useful guideline, from a pamphlet issued by Dinosaur National Monument in Colorado to promote "soft" cycling: "If each of us fears the effects of our impacts on resources more than we fear the law, there will be little need for more regulation."

6 ADVANCED RIDING TECHNIQUES

A curious thing about cycling technique: despite scores upon scores of ergonometric studies and experiments, some dating as far back as the mid-1800s and the infancy of the bicycle, cycling has never had anything like a Bible of technique, an irrefutable book of knowledge. Cycling has never had a god-like personage such as Bobby Jones, who showed up in the 1920s to settle forever issues relating to the proper way to swing a golf club.

Instead, the subtle methods of effective cycling have become established more through anecdote, word-of-mouth, and presumption than through empiricism. Capable riders figure out something that works for them, and, talking a good ball game, pass along what is often misguided advice to others. This convolution of information has no doubt arisen because cycling, as simple an activity as it might seem, brings together a remarkably complex set of variables relating to the rider, the bike, and the terrain. What is effective for one rider on a certain kind of bike in certain conditions might be utter foolishness for another rider under different circumstances.

The bicycle, unlike a golf club, baseball bat, or tennis racket, isn't just some *utensil*. It's a machine that springs into life as soon as a rider puts it in motion. The bike reacts both to the inconsistencies of the someone else might not work for you, and vice versa. In fact, as you experiment—as you should—with different techniques in your riding, you might hit upon some deft and subtle trick of your own. Unknown and untried elsewhere in the cycling world, it can become your personal bit of technique magic, a sliver of knowledge that you can pass along to others in the continuing evolution of cycling methodology. Nevertheless, you'll expedite your rise up the learning curve by at least starting with fundamental techniques that have already been proved to be effective.

Drafting—following in the slipstream of a lead rider to lessen wind resistance—can reduce your workload by as much as 30 percent. Notice that the following riders are angled to the right of the leader, suggesting that the wind is coming slightly from the left.

riding terrain and the unique impulses of each rider. What's more, riding techniques have evolved as both bikes and the terrain covered by bikes have changed. Tactics for taking on logs and boulders weren't even a consideration until mountain biking came into being and bikes were built to negotiate such gnarly stuff.

All of this points to an inescapable fact: what works for

Riding techniques in this chapter are divided between techniques for riding the road and for mountain biking. But all are grounded in solid riding fundamentals, so you might want to review Chapter 4 before moving onward.

RIDING THE ROAD

Warding off the Wind

DRAFTING. How nice it is, when riding into a headwind, to have friends to ride with. The lessening of wind resistance through drafting, or slipstreaming behind another rider, can reduce your workload by as much as 30 percent.

That's the good news. The bad news is that drafting can be risky business. The benefits of drafting are significant only when you're riding with your front wheel within a foot of another rider's rear wheel. The slightest change in direction or speed can lead to a touch of wheels and a crash. In fact, the Adventure Cycling Association, the nonprofit tour organizer, prohibits drafting on its multiday tours.

Still, drafting can be fun, efficient, and relatively safe when done right. For starters, never sneak up on someone else's wheel. Always alert a rider ahead of you that you're in a drafting position. Use your brakes sparingly, and if the rider ahead of you slows, pull right or left (if there is room available) and drift alongside the other rider rather than slamming on the brakes. A great way to make enemies when drafting with a group is to be brake-happy. And don't become fixated on the wheel of the rider in front of you. For safety's sake, keep an alert eye on the road ahead, focusing over and around the back of the lead rider. That way you'll be able to anticipate changes in speed rather than simply react to what the rider in front of you does.

DID YOU KNOW

The propeller used to generate wind in a wind tunnel for testing cycling aerodynamics at Texas A&M University is a hand-me-down from Enola Gray, the plane infamous for dropping the atomic bomb on Hiroshima.

Finally, know when drafting is a good idea and when it isn't. Drafting is great on flat, paved surfaces and gentle climbs. But it's a hazard on a fast downhill, since gravity is already providing a big push. It's also a dumb idea most of the time in mountain biking, where speed and direction changes occur often and where loose debris spewing from the lead rider's wheel can be injurious.

THE PACELINE. There is, by the way, an etiquette in drafting: share the load. It is a socialist concept, the idea of sharing work for the common good. The lead rider "pulls" for a minute or less—perhaps just a few seconds in a large group—then drifts to the side, allowing a new rider to take the lead. The former leader eases back to rejoin the group at the back.

The process continues, each rider taking a turn in the lead, until eventually the original leader is back in front. This rotating procession is what's called a paceline, and when you get the hang of it, it's an utter gas—the synergy of cycling elevated to the level of group experience. Make sure to begin reaccelerating smoothly *before* drifting back to the last rider in the pack; that way you'll be able to slide comfortably onto the end of the line, rather than having to sprint suddenly to catch up.

Smooth Climbing

STICKING WITHIN YOUR LIMITS. Climbing can be a rewarding part of riding or it can be hellish pain and misery. The key to achieving the former rather than suffering the latter is ridiculously simple: Learn your limits. Mike Engelman, former U.S. Cycling Team member and one of the world's best climbers, puts it this way: "Approach climbing as a mental exercise. Ride with yourself, not against yourself."

On a steep climb, it is a hair's breadth that separates a comfortable pace and a pace that can quickly turn you into a wasted, panting, red-faced mess. Unlike riding on flatland or downhills, climbing doesn't afford the luxury of coasting as a quick way of recovering from pushing too hard. Once you go into oxygen debt—that is, once your lungs can't deliver enough oxygen to keep the muscles going (see Chapter 8)—you're pretty much history on a climb.

To hold off oxygen debt—to stay within your limits—stick with these three rules: (1) ride in a gear that allows you to maintain, for a long stretch, the cadence close to what you normally ride on the flats; (2) make sure to keep your stroke smooth and round, taking advantage of every part of the pedaling orbit in applying pressure; (3) stay relaxed.

STAYING STEADY. Number 1 should be clear—if you're thrashing around to keep up your cadence, shift to a lower gear. Do this *before* you start struggling; the slower your cadence when going uphill, the harder it is to shift gears effortlessly, and only a half dozen struggling strokes in the wrong gear can be enough to initiate a journey into oxygen debt. As Engelman says, "Your speed on long climbs isn't as important as keeping your effort steady."

GOING FULL CIRCLE. Number 2 may take practice, so try it on the flats before hitting the hills. Work on initiating pressure on the pedals just past the twelve-o'clock position, and begin pulling back easily on the pedals (if you have cleats or toe clips) at the five-o'clock position. Don't force the action: applying pressure incorrectly on one pedal can actually add resistance on the other, and you'll end up increasing your workload rather than lessening it. A lot of experienced climbers like to shift backward slightly in the saddle when climbing. While this diminishes somewhat the amount of downward force they can apply between the two- and five-o'clock position, it makes applying pressure at other points in the pedaling orbit slightly easier.

THE MIND GAME. Number 3 is more a mental process than a physical one—or a mental process that begets a phys-

When touring through gently rolling terrain, it's often easier to maintain a fluid rhythm by standing up and riding a high gear uphill, rather than breaking your rhythm by shifting gears constantly.

ical one. Impatience is probably the climber's worst enemy. Eager to get to the top and to get the climb over with—or impatient with the slow pace that climbing dictates—these impatient climbers will push themselves to anaerobic breakdown. As they find themselves struggling, they compound their problems by working even harder to overcome their struggling, wasting energy that could have been used to keep the bike rolling and adding to the difficulty of the climb.

ENERGY CONSERVATION. How important marshaling your energy reserves is when climbing! Says Betsy King, a former U.S. national champion in several events: "Saving every fraction of a percent of muscular effort makes a huge difference on a ride with several climbs." That's why you rarely see the great climbers moving their upper bodies much. Instead, they find a position on the bike in which they can stay most relaxed and stick with it. Since going uphill is relatively slow, causing minimal wind resistance, an aerodynamic posture is less important than a relaxed posture. That's why many good climbers sit upright in the saddle—it's simply more comfortable.

If you do move your upper body—something you'll probably want to do when you stand up to stretch your back and legs while climbing—do so primarily as a means of releasing tension, rather than as a means of trying to add body leverage to pushing the pedals. Think of it as dancing on the pedals—an easy, rhythmic swaying, not a grunting bump-and-grind. In the process, your bike may sway slightly

Above: On steep hills rocking back and forth gently as you pedal in a standing position delivers extra power to your stroke and keeps your muscles from locking up. Don't overdo the motion: On the down stroke, keep your hip over (not outside) your foot. Opposite: Great form, great scenery.

from side to side, counterbalancing your swaying motion. That's fine, but don't overdo it; swaying increases tire-road friction, increasing your workload.

One last thing about climbing: When you get to the top, dig it. Soak up the scenery and the fruits of your effort. Reaching the summit is the reward for a job well done, so enjoy it to the fullest.

Taking on Turns

Brake before a turn, lean into the turn, avoid oversteering, and keep your outside leg extended. That is good cornering technique in a nutshell, both for road riding and mountain biking. The first three principles might seem obvious, although mountain bikers, at slower speeds and on rougher terrain, might find the need to steer the front wheel—that is, directing the front wheel by manipulating the handlebars—on occasion.

STEERING STRAIGHT. The idea is still to avoid *over*steering, even when mountain biking. Oversteering upsets balance and at high speeds can send your rear wheel into a tailspin. In most cases, if you have entered a turn at an appropriate speed, leaning into it will get you through. Leaning into the turn keeps you balanced over the bike and keeps the front and rear wheels tracking on approximately the same arc, lessening the chance of a spill.

EXTEND YOUR OUTER LEG. Extending the outer leg is a simple technique that even experienced riders often forget. Again, this position is essentially a

Classic cornering form: Outer leg extended, leaning in, inside knee turned out for extra balance, upper body driving aggressively through the turn. Notice that there is almost no steering of the front wheel by turning the handlebar.

way of remaining balanced—or counterbalanced, to be precise, as you lean into the turn. Extending your outer leg also ensures that your inner pedal is at its high point, preventing the possibility of the pedal striking the pavement or trail as you lean in.

Don't be timid about pushing your weight slightly forward and inside through a turn; getting your weight and momentum traveling forward through the arc of the turn is a way of counteracting the centrifugal force pulling you outward. For the same reason, you'll want to pedal out of the turn as the bike begins to plumb back to an upright position.

Going Down

Going downhill is all about speed control, and speed control is all about strategic braking—or being prepared to brake. That entails riding in a stable and balanced position—feet horizontal (in the three and nine o'clock positions), weight shifted slightly back in the saddle, upper body relaxed, and hands on the brakes, prepared to compress when necessary.

CHECKING SPEED. When it's time for a speed check, brake lightly, increasing pressure gradually as you need it. Subtle braking is much more important when going downhill than on the flats, since you're working against the added force of gravity. Brake suddenly, and your body—its mass overloaded by the effects of gravity—will end up on the wrong side of your handlebars. If you can, try to brake on flatter stretches, where that extra gravitational pull is minimal, rather than on steep drop-offs. Avoid "riding" your brakes, especially on long descents. Your brake pads will overheat and your hands will quickly grow sore and numb.

Work your way up to higher down-

Going downhill is all about being prepared to brake before you need to, and subtly checking your acceleration by squeezing the brakes lightly. Be especially alert when riding in the rain. since water on the rims makes brakes less responsive.

RIDING IN THE RAIN

Be prepared, be cautious, and don't sweat getting wet. Being prepared means bringing rain gear if there's a chance the skies might open. Even on warm days, the cool rain against your exercise-warmed body can lead to hypothermia—a risk exacerbated by the cooling effect of the breeze generated by riding.

Being cautious means being aware of how rain can dramatically change the character of any riding surface. Rocks become slippery, mud develops. A thin, greasy patina develops on tar roads, while metal-grid bridges become virtual skating rinks. So what do you do? Simple—you slow down, especially around corners and going downhill. Being cautious also means allowing extra braking distance, since wheel rims and brake pads are not nearly as responsive when wet as when dry. Periodically applying your brakes lightly, even when you don't have to, is a good way of clearing excess moisture but is no assurance of being able to brake quickly when necessary.

One last recommendation: wipe your chain down thoroughly after a ride in the rain. A little bit of moisture can go far in making a chain squeaky, cranky, and unsupple.

hill speeds that involve less braking. You may never develop the confidence to hit 60 miles an hour, as riders do in races like the Tour de France. But you should feel confident accelerating—on straight, open descents, to at least 30 mph—and feel just as confident applying your brakes, in a controlled and balanced way, when traveling at that speed.

DID YOU KNOW

The world endurance record for sustaining a wheelie is 5 hours, 21 minutes, set by Californian Kurt Osburn.

MOUNTAIN BIKING

On the Rise

Steepness and surface variability are the twin elements that differentiate mountain-bike climbing from climbing on the road. The basic principles still apply—maintain a smooth, round stroke, stay relaxed, keep your cadence up—but steep, rough riding has a way of playing havoc with your sense of balance and control.

GEARING SMALL. This is where those little gears really come into play. If the surface is especially rough or loose, shift to an even lower gear than you're normally comfortable with—a gear choice that will force you to increase your cadence to as high as 90 rpm. This will allow you to maintain forward (or upward) momentum when you encounter obstacles such as rocks, logs, or loose dirt. Because your forward momentum is already minimal on a steep climb, it doesn't take much of an obstacle to inflict a stall-out. By being in a gear that you can spin fast and easily, you increase your chances of pedaling right over, past, or through those obstacles.

On steep climbs, subtlety of body movement is your greatest ally, just as it is in road riding. In other words, relax, minimize upper-body movement, and be patient. You'll eventually get to the top of the climb, so don't rush things. When you try to push too hard, two things typically happen. The rear wheel spins out from the extra torque produced by sudden force on the pedals, and the front wheel lifts as you yank the handlebars in search of extra leverage against the pedals. Next thing you know, you're at a dead stop or, worse, you've flipped over backward.

Alan Coté, a seasoned racer and bike tester for *MTB*, a leading mountain-biking magazine, recommends staying low and slightly forward in the saddle for steep climbs. That position will help you maintain your balance, in turn making it easier to maintain a smooth, easy stroke, and will also keep the front wheel on the ground.

DISMOUNTING. Last but not least, when the going gets really steep and gnarly, no honor is lost in dismounting and walking. Even in races, competitors often take on difficult parts of a course on foot, with bikes slung over their shoulders. And if your fellow riders call you a wimp, tell them you've got scientists to back you up. According to Frank Rowland Whitt and David Gordon Wilson in *Bicycling Science,* "At gradients of 20 percent there is no really appreciable advantage of riding the bicycle, even in a low gear."

Ned Overend, one of the world's best mountain bikers, demonstrates good and bad climbing form. Top: By pushing his butt back and his shoulders forward, he is pushing forward and at the same time distributing his weight evenly. Bottom: Here he is standing up and pulling backward, a less efficient stance. Notice how his front wheel is beginning to lift off the ground.

EXTREME TECHNIQUE

WHEELIE TIMES

Once you've developed excellent riding skills, you may be ready to pull off a front wheelie, here made to look almost easy by world-famous mountain-bike stunt-meister Hans Ray. Not recommended for the faint of heart.

Going Down

KAMIKAZE DOWNHILLING. While going downhill is just another part of road riding, it's an altogether different matter in mountain biking. Descending is what many mountain bikers live for. It is a test of athleticism, bike handling skills, daring, and downright craziness.

Top: Hans Ray, famous for his agility and balance in handling a mountain bike, demonstrates textbook form in negotiating a supersteep downhill pitch: rear end well behind the saddle, feet maintaining a horizontal position on the pedals, arms extended, hands over brake levers. Bottom: Meanwhile, even the experts aren't perfect. Mountain-bike champ John Tomac is too far forward, with his chin ahead of the handlebars. If he brakes hard, he's cruising for a bruising.

Don't forget to maintain your momentum through a turn, even if the riding surface is loose or rough. A heavy hand on the brake when negotiating such a turn is as likely to lead to a crash as going too fast.

is a fine one on a steep, twisting, rugged descent. There is no substitute for skill—a product of experience—in maintaining control, and there is no substitute for stupidity—in the form of overconfidence or overzealousness—in courting chaos.

The truly gonzo downhillers get their thrills by pushing the limits of risk, and when sitting in conversation among hard-core mountain bikers, you're apt to hear a litany of war stories. Blood, broken bones, ruined bikes—life on and beyond the edge of cycling risk can make a gonzo biker's day.

Another way of putting this is that the line between control and calamity

The key to becoming a good downhiller is to develop your skills slowly, gradually working up to speed. That may take some discipline, especially when others you're riding with leave you in the dust. All that means is they're either more skillful or crazier than you.

SENSIBLE DOWNHILLING. You need just two things to be able to descend

TECHNIQUE TIP

BRAKING BEFORE TURNING

Using your brakes properly is essential to avoiding wipe-outs when turning, especially on steep downhills. Ned Overend, 1990 mountain-biking world champion, uses his front brake sparingly, mostly before reaching the turn. "When I'm going downhill, I look for a smooth or straight spot before the turn for applying the front brake," says Overend. "Then when I'm making the turn, almost all of my brake pressure is on the rear wheel." Too much front-brake pressure while making the turn can result in the rear wheel spinning out, or the rider (you) going over the handlebars.

TECHNIQUE TIP

THE BUMP THRUST

The world is a bumpy place, and the world of mountain biking is often an incredibly bumpy place. Bumps, ranging from pavement seams on the road to logs across a trail, can be jarring interruptions at best and crash causers at worst. But there is a way of taking the jar out of the bump—call it the bump thrust.

The bump thrust is a way of pushing and throwing—*thrusting*—the bike over a bump. When you see a bump ahead, stop pedaling and allow yourself to feel light in the saddle. For a particularly large bump, you might want to stand up on the pedals to help absorb the jolt. As you approach the bump, give a quick push to the handlebars to accelerate the front wheel and lighten its load, helping it to roll smoothly over the bump.

As you get good at this technique, you can add lift to it for larger obstacles. (1) As you lurch your body back, simultaneously yank up on the handlebars. As the front wheel clears the log (2), move your body forward to help the rear wheel over, but make sure not to grab the front brakes in the process. Now, with your weight centered (3), keep up your momentum by giving a push on the pedals.

Mountain-bike champ John Tomac, displaying textbook climbing form—butt back and shoulders pushing forward, his weight evenly distributed to keep his front wheel from lifting off the ground—keeps riding where others are forced to walk.

confidently—balance and speed control. In order to get into a balanced position for a descent, start by standing on your pedals, with the pedals on a horizontal plane. You don't have to stand tall, just tall enough to be above your saddle so that you can comfortably absorb jolts with your legs.

Next, shift your hips back slightly on a gentle descent and even farther back as the pitch steepens. On extremely steep descents, skilled riders end up with their butts well behind the saddle and over the rear wheel. You might find that position awkward and you may not need it until

TECHNIQUE TIP

TAKE A HIKE

Who says you always have to ride when riding? On extremely steep hills, the best thing to do may be to stop pedaling and start walking your bike. Even the world's best riders occasionally walk, including Juli Furtado, two-time world and four-time national mountain-biking champion. "Even in races, I'll sometimes get off and walk," says Furtado. "When it's really steep, walking is often the wisest thing to do to save energy."

you encounter truly steep grades, exceeding, say, 20 percent. But experiment with it and get comfortable with it on moderate descents. That way you won't freak out—or will be less likely to freak—when you hit the super steeps and the rumble-seat position becomes essential.

Keep your body aligned evenly (side to side) over the frame, just as you would in your basic riding posture. A centered body position is especially important on a very steep descent when you're moving very slowly and can't accelerate as a way of regaining balance. If you aren't centered, you stand a good chance of toppling over sideways.

Staying Balanced

Some riders like to pull their knees in, to the point where they are almost touching, as a way of keeping their alignment centered. Avoid swinging your shoulders or hips from side to side; try to remember that you and your bike are supposed to be a synergistic unit, not two elements coincidentally moving in the same direction. That might be difficult when you have to steer around corners and obstacles. The trick, again, is not to *over*steer; avoid jerking the handlebars with your hands or making sudden movements with your upper body. Think of yourself as flowing downhill, like a stream seeking a path of least resistance.

As in climbing—or in any other phase of mountain biking—don't feel that your personal honor has been besmirched if you dismount to walk around a particularly steep or tricky

TECHNIQUE TIP

SHOULDERING THE LOAD

When slinging your bike over your shoulder—as mountain bikers must do from time to time—sling it over your right shoulder. That will keep the drivetrain away from your body, keeping your clothing free of chain grease and avoiding nasty scratches from the chain-ring teeth.

RIDING INDOORS

No way around it: riding indoors on a stationary rig is tedious. But for many people who live in wintry climates, it's the best way to stay in riding shape when the cold weather sets in. So if you're willing to put up with this tedium, make the most of it. Perhaps the best setup is a set of rollers—the cycling version of a treadmill—on which you can vary the resistance against the wheels. Cycling machines (such as Lifecycles) or "trainers," which suspend the rear wheel off the ground, allow you to turn pedals to stay in shape, but the demands placed on your riding technique and balance are minimal. Riding on rollers, on the other hand, is still real riding, requiring good form, concentration, and balance.

Dr. Steve Johnson, director of the Human Performance Research Laboratory at the University of Utah, strongly recommends that when riding indoors, you use fans to cool you down. Sweat only cools the body, Johnson says, when it evaporates. If your T-shirt is soaked and your hair is drenched in sweat, you might feel like you're getting a better workout, but the lack of evaporation, says Johnson, leads quickly to "thermal destruction."

Whatever your indoor riding method, do anything to relieve the tedium. Turn up the stereo. Watch TV (very common). Listen to books on tape (less common). Watch your girlfriend or boyfriend dance (highly uncommon, but very sexy). Tell jokes to yourself. *Anything*. Riding indoors is all about sweating a lot and going nowhere. If you don't do something to energize that dull process, your indoor-riding rig will quickly become a dusty relic.

section of trail. Walking and toting your bike is a perfectly respectable part of mountain biking.

Braking

The truly skilled brakers are those with an intuitive feel for their bikes and the terrain—they have a gift for knowing just when to apply the brakes, how firmly, and for how long. Braking is all about knowing exactly where that fine line lies between control and calamity—and knowing that the line is always changing. Effective braking is a matter of knowing when *not* to brake as much as when to brake.

BEING PREPARED. When you encounter an obstacle—a log, a deep puddle, a rock—your instinct might warn you to slow down, but in fact you'll need forward momentum, not deceleration, to carry you smoothly beyond the obstacle. Anticipation is the key here. You want to brake to a very slow speed before the obstacle so that you can accelerate comfortably over the obstacle itself.

Real mad-dog descenders—such as those who got mountain biking started in Marin County, California, in the late 1970s—have been known to burn brake pads and ruin wheel bearings in long, fast descents. Neither should happen if you control your speed properly. Part of the secret is working the brakes lightly, on and off, not riding or hammering the brakes. Speed can mount quickly on steep descents, so regularly tap the brakes as a way of checking your speed. On very steep hills, you'll probably want to apply more pressure to the rear brake than the front brake; too much front-brake pressure can send you over the handlebars. You don't, however, want to apply too much rear-brake pressure; it will cause your rear wheel to fishtail.

World Cross-Country Champion Ruthie Matthes demonstrates good cornering technique on a steep descent by extending her left knee outward for extra stability, extending her right leg fully, and keeping her weight well back with her stomach over the saddle. She maintains momentum by driving the front wheel forward. Note the full extension of her arms.

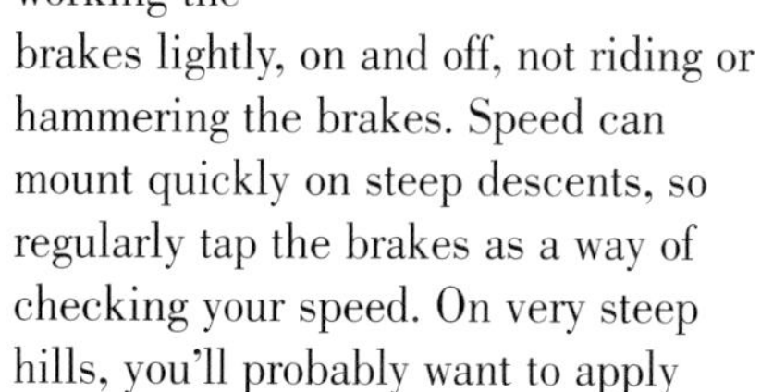

TECHNIQUE TIP

GETTING UP TO GET DOWN

"A critical thing about going downhill is to establish a low center of gravity," says Ned Overend, 1990 mountain-biking world champion. Ironically, the way to get your center of gravity lower is to stand up out of the saddle. By standing, most of your weight is on the pedals, while if you remain sitting, most of your weight rests higher up on the saddle.

PICKING YOUR SPOTS. Finally, always factor in the riding surface when calculating braking distances. You may do well to pick your braking spots for speed control. Gravel on back roads, for example, can be treacherous and lead to spinouts. If possible, look for a patch of smooth, hard—and dry—dirt, rather than braking on loose surfaces.

The Early Shift

Plenty has already been said about shifting gears, but one point needs to be reiterated for mountain bikers: *anticipate*. Look far ahead for sudden, steep uphills and shift before it's necessary. Spinning a low gear a little faster than you're used to for a few seconds is certainly preferable to stalling out in too high a gear when you start climbing.

You'll by now have noticed one of three words sneaking into almost every sentence: anticipation, balance, and control—the ABCs of cycling. Go ahead and try whatever wacky way of riding moves you, both literally and figuratively. As long as you stick to the ABCs, it's hard to go too far wrong.

?

DID YOU KNOW

How American Lance Armstrong prepared for the 104-degree heat of Greece that racers faced during the 1994 World Road Championships? "I drank a lot of water the days before, up until my urine was clear," Armstrong told *Velo-News,* the bike racing journal. Lesson: If you're anticipating a long, hard ride in extreme heat, start drinking plenty of water long before you hit the saddle to be sure your body is completely saturated.

7 HITTING THE ROAD (OR TRAIL)

The world beckons. All of terra firma is divided in two parts: places where bikes can go and places where they can't, with the first category substantial enough to make the second not worth worrying about, especially since the advent of mountain biking. To be sure, there are places, for either safety, legal, or environmental reasons, where bikes can go but shouldn't, and you should review Chapter 5 to be clear on that score. But that still leaves plenty of room to ride.

The limits of imagination are your only real barrier. You could ride 10 laps around the block near your home (imagination level: low), or you could plot out a new mountain-biking route across Siberia (imagination level: off the scale and wildly ambitious, but not unthinkable). The availability of time, physical fitness, and your avidity for cycling will help you focus in on the types of rides, within those extremes, that are right for you.

If there is one guideline to go by, it is this: stick within your capabilities. As the curtain is raised to expose the world accessible on two wheels, ambition may soar. Possible rides cry out to be ridden. But if you're just getting back in the saddle after a long layoff or have been riding irregularly—if you're still thick around the midsection or unsure of your bike-handling skills—lofty ambitions could lead you astray.

This is a matter of safety as

Chapter 8 for details on how your body works when cycling and what you can do to get it to work better.) Aim toward finishing your rides feeling refreshed, buzzing with an endorphin rush, rather than exhausted.

Ski resort rides, like this one at Deer Valley, Utah, aren't necessarily made less scenic by the presence of ski lifts.

EVERYDAY RIDES

Chapter 10 will delve further into questions of whom to ride with and how to make room to ride (that is, *time* to ride) in your daily schedule. The focus here is on the where and what of a good ride: where should you go? And what kind of ride—long or short, straight or looped, for an hour, a day, a week, or longer—should you plan on?

much as anything else. Statistically, most cycling accidents occur late in a ride, when the rider is weary and concentration and balance falter. And with the extra measure of safety usually comes an extra measure of enjoyment. A sense of accomplishment is a far more satisfying feeling at the end of a ride than is that whipped feeling of dejection that comes with coming up short.

So start modestly and build up, physically and psychologically, to bigger and better rides. (Refer to

Where to Go . . .

On a very basic level, you answered this question when you chose a bike at the shop. You've determined in choosing a certain type of bike the kind of terrain you're likely to—and *want* to—encounter. Now it's time to

Standard road maps are usually adequate for plotting a road ride. For more cycling-specific maps or guidebooks, check with your local bike shop.

get down, perhaps quite literally, to the nitty-gritty of where to ride.

Good resources for finding ideal routes are local bike clubs, bike shops, and chambers of commerce. Bike clubs can recommend routes regularly used by their members. Good bike shops are almost always staffed with enthusiastic cyclists, not just sharp salespeople who happen to be working in bike shops, and they're usually eager to share with you some of their favorite rides. They can often give you free route maps and recommend the best road maps for your locale. A number of communities have officially designated bike routes (often marked by signs), and some have gone so far as to create bike maps, which chambers of commerce, public libraries, and tourism offices can usually supply.

. . . FOR ROAD RIDERS. Dream rides involve smooth surfaces, wide, paved shoulders, no traffic, and great scenery. Few rides, of course, score perfect 10s in all categories, so you'll have to determine your own priorities for any particular ride.

Small back roads—those usually marked in blue or gray on a road map—are often sensational for scenery and for that soul-satisfying feeling of being away from the burdens and encroachments of civilization. But they do have drawbacks. They are often poorly maintained, resulting in a rough, uncomfortable ride. Also, they usually lack much of a shoulder, meaning cars must either go around you or you go into a ditch. There might be less traffic than on a more substantial thoroughfare, but each encounter with a car or truck can become a nerve-racking confrontation. If you do

Off-road touring through the Sinks of Gandy area, West Virginia, not far from Canaan.

opt for backroad riding, be especially wary when riding narrow, twisting, shoulder-less roads.

Major roads usually have substantial shoulders, often smoothly paved. You still need to be vigilant, since even the most smoothly paved shoulder can present problems, broken glass and the remnants (sand, gravel) of winter road maintenance being common. Yet despite such lurking hazards, the wide and smoothly paved shoulder is one of the safest and most pleasant surfaces to ride.

With trucks and cars roaring by at considerable speed, you might feel you're sacrificing some critical aesthetic value in your riding. Still, not all major roads are inundated with rude traffic and commercial strips. Major roads that connect population centers, rather than go through population centers, are often good choices.

. . . FOR MOUNTAIN BIKERS. Single track or double track, steep or gentle, aerobic or acrobatic. Devoted mountain bikers dream of rides combining all those things, but every rider has priorities. One thing to remember is that "mountain biking" is a very loose and often misapplied term. While industry statistics are weak on this point, it is generally agreed that most bikes sold as "mountain bikes" never leave paved roads. So in the absence of any better definition, consider mountain biking to refer here to any riding off of paved surfaces.

If you are new to mountain biking, start with unpaved roads (aka "double track") and work your way up to one-lane trails (aka "single-track"). Riding on roads usually offers a chance to do longer rides, hence helping to build up your aerobic fitness. It will also allow you to practice on forgiving terrain some of the techniques—braking, balancing, and so on—you'll need to have fine-tuned for single-track riding. Hard-packed dirt is probably the best surface to seek out; soft dirt gets muddy and rutted, while loose gravel can wreak havoc on your ability to turn and brake smoothly.

Maps for Mountain Bikers

Finding unpaved roads may be easier said than done. Most basic road maps—state or city maps—omit smaller roads. As a result, a local bike shop or bike club is probably an even more important route-finding resource for mountain bikers than for road riders, who still have road maps to fall back on.

The publication of mountain-biking maps and guidebooks is a burgeoning business these days, rushing to catch up with the exploding interest in the sport. But such books and maps usually have limited and

A small pack mounted on your handlebars is just the place for maps, guidebooks, and snacks. And a compass may come in handy in the backcountry.

TECHNIQUE TIP

ELBOW ROOM

If you find yourself fighting the wind on a long ride, make an effort to pull your elbows in. Wind-tunnel tests have shown that there is a significant reduction in wind resistance when cyclists simply pull their elbows in to align with their hands.

spotty distribution. Don't expect to walk into a bookstore and find an appropriate guide or map, as you'll probably have better luck finding one—where else?—in a bike shop. Hiking guides and maps, which are far more plentiful, may be of some help, at least in orienting you to the lay of the land. But these should be used sparingly in planning precise routes, given that mountain bikers are personae non gratae on many hiking trails. Forest Service maps or topographic maps can also be useful in showing secondary roads and topographical contours, if not necessarily roads and trails where mountain bikers do and don't have the right of way.

Farm roads afford great access to the backcountry, here in Highland County, western Virginia not far from the West Virginia line. Be sure to seek the permission of landowners before trespassing.

How Far?

GOING IN CIRCLES. Looped rides are ideal; you can simply vary the distance of your rides by varying the number of loops. If you're on the road, it's best to ride loops in a clockwise direction, minimizing the need to cross traffic.

"Out and back" rides can be trickier. Many cyclists, feeling flushed and sprightly early in a ride, get into a rhythm that carries them well beyond a sensible turn-around point. Then suddenly they realize they've lost track of their math, having forgotten that every mile ridden in one direction adds a mile to the return ride. Somewhere on the return trip they hit the wall and end up struggling to the finish. So on an out-and-back ride, make sure to turn around while you're still feeling fresh.

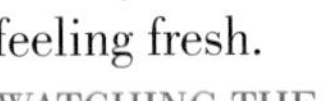

WATCHING THE WIND. Also—especially on out-and-back rides—note the strength and direction of the wind. Tailwinds are sneaky, beguiling you into believing that there's no wind at all. You're sailing along 5 mph faster than you usually ride, obliviously wanting to believe that you've suddenly raised your fitness and cycling ability a notch. Then you turn into the headwind to face physical and psychological defeat. So be guided in your ride by wind—flags, wavy grasses, and, of course, weather vanes work well—and plan your ride accordingly. In places like the prairies, where strong winds are common, experienced riders try to plan rides going into the wind early, when they're fresh, and returning with a tailwind, when they welcome the extra push.

Keeping Up to Speed

Critical to determining how far to ride on the road is coming to terms with a pace you can sustain comfortably for the long haul. For the recreational touring cyclist, that will probably be somewhere in the 12 to 16 mph range. A well-conditioned cyclist can average 16 to 20 mph, while racers may average 25 mph on training rides. Terrain and weather conditions, as well as your (presumably) improving fitness level, will dictate when you can push your pace and when to back off.

Pace, or average speed, means little to mountain bikers. While road riders tend to measure rides by mileage, mountain bikers typically measure rides by time. In mountain biking there are too many ups and downs in the terrain, too many variations in the riding surface. In fact, it's potentially dangerous as a mountain biker to feel a need to maintain a certain pace. You can end up rushing yourself when the terrain dictates caution, especially on tricky downhills; next thing you know, your bike is on top of you, rather than the other way around.

This can make planning a mountain bike ride a little trickier. A ride that took two hours one day might take three another due to changes in weather or surface conditions. So the key is to build plenty of extra time into your ride. If you finish a ride a half hour quicker than planned, so what? Go home, have a beer, go fishing. That's a lot better than ending up mired on the trail, exhausted and fighting to beat the curtain call of daylight.

TECHNIQUE TIP

THE RIDER'S WARDROBE

John Schubert, technical editor for *Adventure Cyclist* magazine, says it's surprising how little clothing you can get by on for a multi-day tour. For riding, Schubert's packing list includes: short-sleeve jersey, arm warmers, two pairs of cycling shorts, leg warmers, long tights, thin, synthetic socks, gloves, and a windbreaker with a draw-string hood. For life on the bike, Schubert's wardrobe includes: swim suit, a couple of pairs of underwear, one pair of long pants, a "half-dressy" shirt, one T-shirt, a long-sleeved wool shirt, and running shoes. Packing only what you really need means less weight to lug around when you're riding.

MULTI-DAY TOURING

More and more people are taking to two wheels as a way of vacationing; the Bicycle Institute of America estimates that roughly 1.8 million Americans went on bike tours or vacations in 1993. That's a modest figure compared to the many millions of Americans who take, say, golf or ski vacations every year. Still, it's more than triple the figure of 10 years earlier, and probably doesn't take accurate account of the many people who now plan vacations around mountain biking.

The Game Plan

ON YOUR OWN. Many people enjoy creating their own itineraries and riding their own rides. You may be among them, and if so, all power to you. But you might also prefer having a tour organizer do the prep work for you, especially if you've never participated in a long tour before. In addition to planning trips, tour organizers also (in most cases) make arrangements for

GEAR TALK

PACKS AND PANNIERS

One of the nice things about touring by bike—as opposed to backpacking—is that you don't need to transport several days of food and gear for an extended trip. The Adventure Cycling Association, the nonprofit tour organizer, suggests that a 30- to 45-pound load is sufficient for most long-distance touring. If you expect to stay in inns or lodges along your route, eliminating the need for camping gear, that load should be significantly lighter.

The question is, how best to carry it? Panniers—cycling "saddle bags"—are the main answer. They are best mounted on a rack over the rear wheel and the best models have a fairly slim profile. The slimmer the panniers, the easier a bike is to handle, the lower the wind resistance, and the less likely you are to snag obstacles in tight spots.

In addition to rear-mounted panniers, a handlebar pack is a great idea, easily accessible for food and gear (tools, rain jacket) you might need while riding. Some handlebar packs come with a clear plastic "envelope" for displaying a map, so you can keep track of where you are on the road. Be sure when you do get a handlebar pack that it doesn't interfere with gear shifting and braking.

If you expect to tote a particularly large load, you can also get a rack and panniers to mount over the front wheels. Be sure when you do pack up that you keep at least 60 percent of your total load in the rear panniers. That will make the bike safer and easier to handle.

Fully packed, with packs and panniers bulging. Keep at least 60 percent of your load in the rear panniers.

meals and lodging. Daily rides are often planned with different riding abilities in mind—shorter and easier routes for less aggressive riders, longer and more challenging rides for the diehards—with everyone ending up at the same destination at day's end. Major tour organizers are listed in the "Sources and Resources" section at the end of this book.

JOINING A TOUR. In many cases, organized tours also include support vans, known in the cycling vernacular as the "sag wagons." A sag wagon can provide mechanical assistance should you have a problem or simply give you a lift should your body quit on you. Actually, if you're arranging your own group tour, you can also arrange to man your own sag wagon. Each member of the group can take a day off to drive the sag wagon, or you can rotate on a half-day basis, switching off at designated lunch spots.

THE GREAT RIDES

Now, as an all-too-brief teaser list, here are a few of the classic rides in America. This is a starter's kit to American bike touring, just to get you thinking about the range of possibilities open to you as a cyclist. Again, refer to the list of tour operators in the "Sources & Resources" section at the end of this book if you want to join an organized tour on any of these rides.

Great Road Rides in the East

BLUE RIDGE, NORTH CAROLINA AND VIRGINIA. Riding the nearly 600 miles that comprise the Blue Ridge Parkway and Skyline Drive is a form of slow and splendid death. No one should undertake this tour without being willing to suffer. Long, steep climbs are the rule of the road on a roadway that spans nearly 6,000 vertical feet. Yet that vertical muscle, swathed in the humidity that gives the Blue Ridge its blueness, makes this as impressive a mountain range as any in the country. Be prepared to encounter traffic along the parkway, especially in midsummer—this is one of the great auto tours as well as bike tours in America.

EVERY CYCLIST'S SURVIVAL KIT

Survival is the key word here—these lists include only the bare essentials. If you've got space in your packs, you can always take more: a book, a Frisbee, or a bottle of wine, for example, might not be essential but can certainly make a ride more fun.

ON ANY RIDE:

Water
Identification
Basic tool kit
Basic first aid kit
Suntan lotion
Sun glasses
Lip balm
Map
Pocket knife
Food (if longer than an hour)
Money

FOR ANY MULTI-DAY RIDE:

2 pairs of cycling shorts
2 or 3 shirts
Noncycling shorts and pants
Fleece pullover, sweat shirt, or wool sweater
2 or 3 pairs of socks
Noncycling shoes
Rain gear
Toiletries
Insect repellent
Soap
Sunscreen

IF YOU PLAN TO CAMP:

Sleeping bag
Tent
Ground cloth
Cooking utensils
Eating utensils
Towel
Toilet paper
Flashlight
Soap

Signing on for a packaged tour with a reputable operator is an ideal way to see a foreign country. What better destination than the lush, rolling landscape of Ireland?

LANCASTER COUNTY, PENNSYLVANIA. Nowhere in America is nonmotorized traffic given more respect than in Pennsylvania Dutch country. The Amish and Mennonite families who live here still resist automation. In the pecking order of road use, cars rank third, behind horse-drawn carriages and bikes. This is popular bike-touring country for good reason: the terrain is perfect, neither flat nor extremely hilly; the scenery is bucolic; and the food is great. Ride hard and then stuff yourself with homemade breads and sausages and local produce.

Great Off-Road Rides in the East

NORTHEAST KINGDOM, VERMONT. This might not be quite off-road territory, but it's certainly off *paved* roads. The dirt roads of the Northeast Kingdom—all small mountains, small lakes, small towns, rustic life—are for leisurely touring, for soaking in the beauty of the countryside passing by. Single-track jocks might be disappointed, but there are plenty of other places in this world for them to get their kicks. Places like the Northeast Kingdom are in short supply in America these days, so don't rush it. Go slow and check into country inns at night. Stare down cows and watch the maple trees act out their autumnal color pageant.

POCAHANTAS COUNTY, WEST VIRGINIA. West Virginia has emerged in recent years as eastern mountain biking's promised land. West Virginia is not

A lookout, Monongahela National Forest, Pocahontas County, West Virginia. The state is among the most popular in the East among mountain bikers.

just hilly—what would you expect of the so-called mountain state?—it's never flat. Mapped out on that up-and-down landscape is an abundance of old farm roads, mining roads, single-track trails—the whole mountain-bike shooting match. The climbs and descents you find here might not be as long as in the Rockies, but they can be exceedingly steep and bone-jarring,

TECHNIQUE TIP

RELAX THAT GRIP

You might think, quite logically, that holding onto the handlebars is a basic part of riding. Not quite so—think instead of the handlebars as a place to rest your hands, not something to hold onto. Many riders have a tendency to grip the bars too tightly, increasing that grip to a vise-like clench when working hard on a long climb. The result, compounded on long rides, is tension stored in the upper body and soreness in the hands, arms, and shoulders. That in turn can severely impair your ability to deliver a smooth and relaxed stroke to the pedals. So rest your hands on the bars, gripping only when you need to brake or steer.

the kind of stuff to put your bike-handling skills to a supreme test.

The San Juan Mountains of southern Colorado are great for both road and mountain-bike touring.

Great Road Rides in the Rockies

DURANGO, COLORADO. Actually, there's great riding off-road in this neighborhood, too, so if you're a switch-hitting cyclist, bring both your mountain and road machines. Regardless of what you're riding, the key thing here is the scenery: pound for pound, the San Juans may be the handsomest range in all of the Rockies. But be prepared: the climbs are long and steep and the pass elevations are above 10,000 feet. Don't spoil it all by pushing too hard. Instead, take several days to ride a couple of hundred miles. Bring your fishing rod and your panoramic camera and take your time.

GLACIER NATIONAL PARK, MONTANA. The Going-the-Sun Road in Glacier is itself a brilliant piece of road engineering. Snaking upward from deep valleys to the high-alpine splendor of Logan Pass, its sharp curves hang on near-vertical escarpments of rock and tundra. The strategy here is to rise early and hit the long, steep climb before the road clogs with car traffic during the midday hours. And once you've completed the 26-mile, 3,500-

vertical-foot climb to the summit, it's all downhill—a long coast toward the juncture of vertical mountain upthrust and the horizontal sweep of the prairie.

Great Off-Road Rides in the Rockies

GREAT DIVIDE TRAIL. It's still a work in progress, but how does the idea of a 3,000-mile off-road trip from Canada

THE RESORT REPORT: Ski-Resort Mountain Biking

If you're really gung-ho to sink your teeth into steep and technical single-track riding, ski resorts are great places to start. Many resorts are discovering in mountain biking a summertime windfall to tide them over quite nicely from one winter to the next. Board a ski lift with your bike, and in about the time it takes to say "I'm glad I didn't have to ride up this hill" a hundred times, you're at the summit, ready for a downhill adrenaline rush. And, of course, if you do want to ride up that hill, no one's stopping you.

Perhaps better than simply riding at ski resorts is learning to ride at ski resorts. Several resorts have developed excellent mountain-biking schools and instructional camps for novice, intermediate, and expert riders. The following are leaders of the ski-resort pack, but be sure to call ahead about programs because, in the ever-changing landscape of mountain biking, programs are regularly being changed, improved, expanded, or (alas) even dropped.

CRESTED BUTTE, COLORADO. Crested Butte is one of the real hotbeds of mountain biking. Clinics, camps, week-long mountain-bike vacations—there is always something going on here. For information, call 303-349-2333 or 800-544-8448.

MOUNT SNOW, VERMONT. The Mount Snow Mountain Bike School is probably the best known and arguably the best of its kind in the country. For information, call 800-245-7669.

MAMMOTH MOUNTAIN, CALIFORNIA. The Kamikaze Downhill Race is Mammoth's most famous ride, but riders disinclined to go as fast as possible and hurt themselves should ask about skill-enhancing clinics and camps. For information, call 619-934-2571 or 800-367-6572.

WINTER PARK, COLORADO. If you're just getting started, joining a half-day instructional tour here is a good way to get started on the right foot. After that, there's plenty of terrain here for graduating to bigger and better tours. For information, call Backcountry Biking, 303-726-4812.

Riding by a geyser near the north entrance to Yellowstone National Park.

to Mexico grab you? The first sections of the trail have been designated and mapped in Montana, and the process is moving southward, approximately following the Continental Divide. Bite off as big or little a chunk of the route as you choose, and appreciate the resplendence of the Rockies far from the madding crowds of traffic-spoiled main roads.

MOAB, UTAH. How quickly fame turned to legend, and how quickly legend turned Moab into a mountain-biking rite of passage. The legend is the Slick Rock Trail just outside town, a graduate-level test of bike-handling skills over boulders and rock ledges. Thousands of mountain bikers come to the trail every summer like pilgrims on a hajj. So go ahead and make the requisite Slick Rock ride, then turn your attention to the other trails in the area, through Canyonlands National Park and the surrounding desertscape, that you can have almost all to yourself.

Great Road Rides in the West

CRATER LAKE, OREGON. Crater Lake is certainly the deepest (nearly 2,000 feet) and perhaps the bluest and purest lake in the United States. Rim Drive, the 33-mile national park road that loops the lake, ranks as one of the best one-day rides in America. The road surface is smooth, the hills challenging but never brutal, and the landscape—an eerie natural beauty evolved from a massive volcanic blast—constantly inspiring. RV traffic can get obnoxious, but Crater Lake is not one of America's most visited national parks.

Mammoth Mountain, California, is renowned for its Kamakaze Downhill Race, but offers plenty of opportunities for more relaxed riding too.

If you avoid peak hours and the peak summer season, you should be able to ride in peace. For a multi-day tour through this volcanically sculpted region, head in any direction—north, south, east, or west. You can't lose.

NAPA AND SONOMA VALLEYS, CALIFORNIA. On a Saturday afternoon in summer, Route 29 leading north from Napa is an uninterrupted chain of traffic. All those motorists come for the same reason you'll come by bike—to taste and buy the wines that have made Napa Valley famous. Save your Napa Valley riding for midweek, when the traffic lessens, and do your weekend riding on underpopulated roads through the hills surrounding Lake Berryessa to the northeast. Or head west to Sonoma Valley, a port of call for oenophiles but not nearly the tourist magnet that Napa Valley has become. If you don't do any wine tasting while riding in this region, you're missing the main point of being here. For that reason, riding with a tour group with a sag wagon might be a

?

DID YOU KNOW

Perhaps the toughest mountain-bike race in the world is the "Iditasport," a 200-mile race across snow and ice in Alaska and inspired by the famous Iditarod dogsled race. The winners finish in about 18 hours—at night and wearing headlamps. The race is also open to snowshoers and cross-country skiers.

Makings of a dream ride: a smooth road, no traffic, and a setting such as the California redwoods.

Moab, Utah's famed Slick Rock Trail: a postgraduate test of balance and bike-handling skills.

sensible strategy should you be overly enthusiastic in your tasting.

Great Off-Road Rides in the West

MAMMOTH MOUNTAIN, CALIFORNIA. The downhill race held every year at Mammoth, in which riders reach speeds exceeding 50 miles an hour, is an exercise in pure insanity. You can be a lot more mellow about it, taking your time to soak up the views and terrain that make Mammoth the top ski area of the central Sierras. And if you play your cards right, you'll meet one of the many rabid mountain cyclists of southern California who will turn you on to some other mountain-biking paradise sequestered in the high Sierras.

MARIN COUNTY, CALIFORNIA. There might be better places in California to ride a mountain bike—certainly more remote and scenic areas—but this is mountain biking's birthplace. It is history, by God. In the mid-1970s, a bunch of wacko local folks began screaming down Mount Tamalpais with their old balloon-tired klunkers, and a new concept in cycling was born. But with mountainous terrain abutting the ocean, there is a lot more to do on a mountain bike than just screaming down Mount Tamalpais. And don't miss the many very geared-out mountain-biking types—indication of how serious this youthful sport has become.

8 THE FITNESS FACTOR

"You're not a man, you're a machine." George Bernard Shaw, in *Arms and the Man,* did not intend those words as an exhortation to urge cyclists to higher levels of achievement. But he might as well have.

To conceive of what your body does (and must do) to propel a bike effectively, think of it for the moment in coldly dispassionate terms—alternately as a "human engine" and a "fuel cell," as Frank Rowland Whitt and David Gordon Wilson call it in *Bicycling Science.* Your body on a bike is an engine processing fuel—in short, a machine. To appreciate how that machine operates, you'll need, in effect, to look under the hood, at the inner workings of the human engine.

THE AEROBIC/ANAEROBIC EQUATION

During exercise, your body works in two basic ways, aerobically and anaerobically. The body is working aerobically when it is operating at a pace allowing the cardiorespiratory system—the lungs, heart, and bloodstream—to replenish energy as you go. Anaerobic exercise, on the other hand, exceeds the cardiovascular capacity to replenish the muscles with energy. During extreme anaerobic exercise, the minimal amount of energy stored within the muscles is relied on for short-term use. That energy source is used up very quickly—within a few seconds—at which point the muscles basically

A well conditioned cyclist like John Tomac can ride at a pace pushing him above his aerobic zone for extended stretches.

shut down. The 100-meter dash is the classic anaerobic paradigm: after only 10 or 11 seconds of all-out sprinting, the runner can barely walk another step.

The Aerobic Zone

In most cases—whether road riding or mountain biking—cycling is, or should be, primarily an aerobic exercise. Unless you're a track racer, blasting full speed around the banked walls of a velodrome, you're at your best when cycling at an even, aerobic pace. To be sure, mountain bikers, encountering quick ups and downs and obstacles along the trail, tend to move in fits and starts—anaerobic surges—more than do road riders. Still, mountain bikers, just like road riders, can make the most of what they've got by sticking as much as possible to the aerobic zone.

So what, you ask, is your aerobic zone?

Your heart rate, in number of beats per minute, is the determining

DID YOU KNOW

Marty Nothstein, an American who won two gold medals at the 1994 world track championships, has had his heart rate measured as high as 220 beats per minute. An average athlete usually maxes out somewhere around 180 to 190 beats per minute.

Racers who time their sprints perfectly arrive at the line with their muscles burning from total glycogen depletion, something that happens in a matter of seconds.

factor establishing both your aerobic zone and the point at which you go into anaerobic overdrive. Physiologists start by calculating your maximum heart rate. A standard formula in calculating your maximum heart rate—hardly infallible but reasonably reliable—is to subtract your age from 220. The figure you come up with is more of theoretical than practical value, since at your maximum heart rate, your cardiovascular system is at the point of explosion. But the figure is useful in determining your aerobic zone and where it ends at your anaerobic threshold.

Approximate figures used by most physiologists show that your aerobic zone is somewhere in the range of between 60 and 70 percent of your maximum heart rate. For most people that means somewhere in the range of 120 to 150 beats a minute. When your heart rate rises above that range, you

DID YOU KNOW

Before becoming a world champion cyclist, American Lance Armstrong competed in triathlons. Lesson: To become a good cyclist, you don't have to ride as your only form of exercise. Run. Swim. Play basketball or tennis. Mixing up your exercise will keep you fit and keep you interested in keeping fit.

increasingly rely on anaerobic effort, rather than aerobic effort, to make the pedals go round. That's OK for those short bursts—standing on the pedals for a short, steep rise, for example—when you need a little extra muscular physical effort. You start breathing hard, your heart rate rises rapidly, your muscles burn. If you don't back off, allowing your system to return to an aerobic level, you'll quickly self-destruct, or "blow up" in cycling terminology. Pushing too hard on a hill climb, where the dragging force of gravity won't allow you to ease off the pedals, is a classic inducer of the feared blowup.

Robert Gaggoli—one of the world's shrewdest tactical riders—tries to jump away from the pack. A full-out anaerobic burst like Gaggoli's is impossible to sustain for more than a few seconds. Save your anaerobic bursts for when you need them most, to climb a short, steep hill.

Now your aerobic output isn't just a matter of how fast (as in heart rate) your cardiovascular system is working, but also how productively it is working. In other words, with each heart beat, how much fresh oxygen is getting pumped into the blood stream? Physiologists measure your capacity in this regard in terms of something called maxVO_2 (or VO_2max)—basically a calculation of the volume of oxygen your lungs can deliver at your maximum heart rate. The more fit you are, the more aerobic bang you get per beat of your heart. Or put another way, the fitter you are, the more energy your cardiovascular system can produce with less effort.

oomph. But when nearing 80 percent of your maximum heart rate, you begin reaching your anaerobic threshold.

The Anaerobic Threshold

"Threshold" might imply a crisply delineated barrier. Not quite so. To be approximate and melodramatic about it, the anaerobic threshold is the point at which the chemical forces of evil in your system begin overtaking the chemical forces of good. It is that point where your heart and your breathing work vainly to catch up with your

The bad news is that a large percentage of your aerobic capacity is your genetic inheritance, and you're stuck with that. But the good news is that regular exercise can still pay off handsomely. Ed Burke, America's preeminent cycling physiologist, estimates that an active person can increase his or her maxVO_2 by as much as 25 percent through a regular exercise program, involving more than 100 miles of vigorous riding per week. Furthermore, Burke claims that research has shown that training can push up a person's anaerobic threshold by a whopping 44 percent. Next time you feel yourself withering anaerobically on a hill climb, keep that in mind. There is hope.

THE CHEMICAL SOUL OF THE MACHINE

Whitt and Wilson's reference to the body as a "fuel cell" applies to the complex chemistry of turning food (solid and liquid) into fuel to empower your muscles for pedaling. (Whitt and Wilson call it a process "in which chemical energy is converted directly to mechanical power.") Muscles, of course, don't use food for energy. Your grilled chicken, salad, cereal, or french fries—or whatever enters your mouth and stomach—must be converted, in various stages, into a chemical called adenosine triphosphate. That's ATP for short—the muscles' main chemical source of power.

The Power Source

ATP can be derived from glycogen (a form of carbohydrate stored in small amounts in the muscles) for anaerobic exercise. The muscles can use straight shots of glycogen only for short bursts before the chemistry takes an unpleasant turn. Lacking oxygen, the chemical process begins developing lactic acid, displacing useful ATP in the muscle cells. Lactic acid is the evil element that makes the muscles feel painful and weak and renders them all but impotent. As Burke says, "Excess lactic acid simply shuts down the cellular functions. The result is acute

TECHNIQUE TIP

SLIDING & RIDING

Looking for a good way in winter to stay in shape for cycling? Try skating. Eric Heiden, speed-skating star of the 1980 Olympics, was also an accomplished cyclist who competed in the Tour de France. Connie Carpenter, winner of the 1984 Olympic road race, also competed as a speed skater. Or try cross-country skiing, an off-season sport favored by Greg Lemond. Both skating and skiing are great aerobic activities that exercise muscle groups similar to those used in cycling.

long haul. Assuming there is a sufficient fuel supply in the bloodstream mixing with a sufficient supply of oxygen, the muscles should be able to go on in this way fairly painlessly for well over an hour.

Keep your body's fuel tank full by eating snacks (energy bars, trail mix, and fruit, all good sources of complex carbohydrates) during your ride.

Stoking the Engine

The "body aerobic" suggests an appropriate analogy: like the carburetor of another machine—the car engine—the human machine mixes air—the oxygen provided by the cardiorespiratory system—and

muscle fatigue."

But as long as the lungs and heart can pump oxygen through the system at a rate to match your physical output, the muscles can derive ATP from glucose (a blood-borne form of carbohydrate) and fatty acids in the bloodstream. This is the body aerobic—an efficient fuel cell able to ride for the

fuel to generate power.

FOOD AS FUEL. The fuel favored by the human machine, of course, is food. Given the fact that carbohydrates are the muscles' primary source of ATP, it's hardly a surprise that nutritionists recommend a carbohydrate-loaded diet for fueling aerobic effort. (There are two types of carbohydrates in foods:

simple carbohydrates—basically sugars—and complex carbohydrates, derived largely from grains and vegetables. Because of the way carbohydrates are broken down chemically in the body, the latter are considered a far better fuel source for the aerobic athlete.) Physiologists typically recommend for cyclists (and others engaged in aerobic exercise) a diet of 70 percent carbohydrates, 20 percent fat, and 10 percent protein.

How much food you need depends on how far and how hard you ride. A road rider going at a moderate pace (15 to 18 mph) burns about 10 to 15 calories a minute, or 600 to 900 calories an hour. Obviously, torching calories at that rate will lead to weight loss, a principal fitness objective of many riders. Still, no matter how gung-ho you are to trim off excess weight, you need to replenish your fuel supplies, especially on long rides.

As much as you might like to burn away the layers of fat stored in unsightly places on your body, the fuel cell does a lousy job of tapping stored fat as a quick energy source. If you don't replenish your carbohydrates on a long ride, the fuel cell will eventually run out of fuel—a debilitating process athletes call "bonking." To avoid bonking on a long ride, bring along easy-to-eat, carbohydrate-rich foods. Bananas, cookies, brownies, granola bars, energy bars: all are good choices. You don't need a lot—just enough to keep your fuel tank from going bone-dry.

WATER WISE. Speaking of going bone-

Drinking plenty of water—before and during a ride—is critical to maximizing your performance.

DID YOU KNOW

If you're taking up riding as a way to burn calories, you'd be taking it to an extreme if you followed the lead of Seana Hogan, a winner of the 2,905-mile Race Across America (RAMM). Hogan first turned to riding seriously in 1991 and won the RAMM three years later. She trained as much as 600 miles a week for the race and consumed more than 10,000 calories a day–through a high energy liquid diet–during the race.

DID YOU KNOW

According to bicycle physiologist Ed Burke, the human body uses only about 23 percent of the energy it produces. The rest is lost as heat.

dry . . . Perhaps the most common—and potentially dangerous—cause for a drop in cycling performance is dehydration. Burke estimates that on a hot day, a cyclist can lose as much as 10 pounds of water through sweating.

Water in your system performs two functions critical to your cycling performance. First of all it acts as a coolant, just like a coolant in your car radiator. Just like your car's engine, your body basically blows its stack when it overheats—it's no longer able to function. The fear of a blown stack should be sufficient to encourage you to drink plenty and often while riding.

Water also facilitates the blood in carrying nutrients to the muscles and other parts of the body, while cleansing the cells of such unwanted metabolic by-products as lactic acid. One of the most familiar symptoms of dehydration is muscle cramping, a result of insufficient nutrients and a surfeit of toxins.

How much should you drink? Obviously that depends on how hard you ride and how hot it is. You can start by what is sometimes called "prehydrating," downing two or three large glasses of water about a half hour before riding. Then be sure to drink every 15 minutes or so during your ride, even if you don't feel thirsty; thirst is a notoriously unreliable indicator of water depletion. Finally, drink at least one large glass of water as soon as you get home, especially if it has been a hot day. If, as Burke suggests, it's possible to lose 10 pounds of water, there's no way you can replenish that while riding. There's only one real drawback to overdrinking: you end up needing to relieve yourself more often than usual. On the other hand, if you're rarely making trips to the rest room, chances are your water level is low, calling for water replenishment even if you aren't thirsty.

SHAPING UP

Now it's probably a fair guess that you, as a cycling machine, are carrying a few extra, un-machinelike pounds in nonmechanical places. Obviously, to transform your body into an efficient human engine requires getting in shape. In terms of developing overall fitness, there are few activities better than cycling to accomplish the task.

What the Experts Say

In a survey of fitness experts conducted a few years ago by the President's Council on Physical Fitness, cycling rated second only to running among popular forms of exercise as a well-rounded means of staying fit. (The experts were not asked to factor in such stuff as fun, where cycling surely has running beat by a comfortable margin.) Cycling was deemed a terrific way of developing cardiorespiratory endurance, of developing muscular endurance and strength, and of controlling weight.

Cycling received low grades only in the "flexibility" category, lacking the kind of twisting, turning, and stretching of sports such as swimming or tennis. But the survey was also conducted before mountain biking had established a beachhead on the American recreational front. Certainly the technical bike-handling skills required to negotiate funky backcountry terrain call for a degree of flexibility uncommon in road riding. Maybe if

TECHNIQUE TIP

STANDING UP TO MAMBO

Generally speaking, sitting in the saddle and pedaling smoothly at a cadence of 70 to 90 rpm is the most cardiovascularly efficient way to ride. Standing up to pedal has several drawbacks: it's hard to pedal with a round stroke and it's hard to pedal smoothly at a cadence much above the 60 to 70 rpm range. Also, it is usually more anaerobic, leading quickly to lactic acid buildup.

That said, there are times—especially when losing momentum during a climb—when standing up to pedal makes good sense. Some riders are very good at climbing in a standing position without delivering themselves into lactic distress. Their secret is falling into an easy rhythm—developing a relaxed, mambo-like dance on the pedals.

Three things go into making the dance effective. The first is striding *forward* on the pedals, rather than downward. That helps to keep some of the stroke roundness that is lost in the up-and-down motion of upright pedaling. Second, shift into a higher gear and slow down your cadence. If you try to spin too fast while standing up, the result is usually a sluggish "bottoming out" at the six o'clock position in the pedaling orbit. And if you are able to spin the pedals fast, it makes more sense to do so in the more efficient sitting position. Third, rock *very* gently from side to side as you pedal—a way of keeping your back muscles loose, adding extra bodyweight leverage to each stroke, and maintaining that mambo-like rhythm.

Standing to pedal is great for short spurts, for which you need a little extra pedaling torque, or to stretch muscles occasionally during a long climb. But for most riders it imposes an anaerobic tax. Unless you're particularly adept at the mambo, stand only briefly and return as soon as possible to the more aerobically efficient method of sitting and spinning.

those experts were asked again today, they'd bump cycling up in the flexibility category and give running a run for its most-favored-sport money.

All of this should point up the obvious: if you want to get your human machine into hummingly good shape, the best thing to do it is simply go out and ride. And the best way to do *that* is to develop a regular riding program.

Riding Regularly

When devising any regular exercise program, fitness pooh-bahs typically create elaborate, precisely delineated training schedules. On Monday of the first week, ride 20 miles at a hard pace, on Tuesday . . . and so on, week after week.

PLANNING A PROGRAM. If you are aiming to condition yourself for a specific event—a long tour, a race, a 100-mile "century" ride—a precise training program might make sense. It works because you have a clearly defined goal to work toward. But as often as not, such a schedule is a setup for failure. You push yourself too hard

LOOSENING UP TO RIDE

Before hitting the road or trail, a full stretching regimen is great—if you can squeeze 15 to 20 minutes of stretching time into a tight schedule. If you can't, even five minutes of stretching can yield a big pay-off when it comes to how long and painlessly you can ride.

If you can afford only an abbreviated stretching routine, concentrate on the muscles that typically are put under the most duress during a ride: the quadriceps, the hamstrings, the muscles of the lower back, and the neck muscles. The following stretches are designed for that purpose. For the definitive guide to stretching for all sports and activities, see *Stretching*, by Bob Anderson.

Before you start contorting your body in the ways suggested in these drawings, keep in mind a few guidelines:

- Try to hold each position 15 to 30 seconds.
- Don't bounce or jerk. Stretch as far as you can in an easy and relaxed manner.
- Never stretch to the point where it hurts, only to the point where the muscles feel tight.
- If you've got time, do the same stretching routine after riding.

NECK & SPINE

Sit on the floor with your right leg straight. Cross your left foot over your right knee and rest it on the floor. Then rest your right one day to attain your target mileage, and riding turns from fun into pain. Or you fail to attain your target, start doubting your commitment to keeping on schedule, grow lax, and ultimately stop riding altogether.

This should not necessarily discourage you from devising a specific schedule. If you respond to that kind of orderliness—in fact, you may require it for motivation, as many people do—sit down and create for yourself a day-by-day, week-by-week training chart. But in terms of getting fit, what you write down on paper means nothing: what matters is the effort you end up putting in on the road or trail.

Any ride, no matter how brief or nonaggressive, is a good ride, but any ride shorter than 30 minutes, especially at low (nonaerobic) intensity levels, does little to improve your overall fitness. If you want to get into good shape—for living life as well as riding your bike—you'll want to increase your cardiorespiratory efficiency. The only way to do that is to

---

elbow on the outside of your left knee. Now, with your left hand resting on the floor behind you, slowly turn your head to look over your left shoulder.

HAMSTRINGS & LOWER BACK

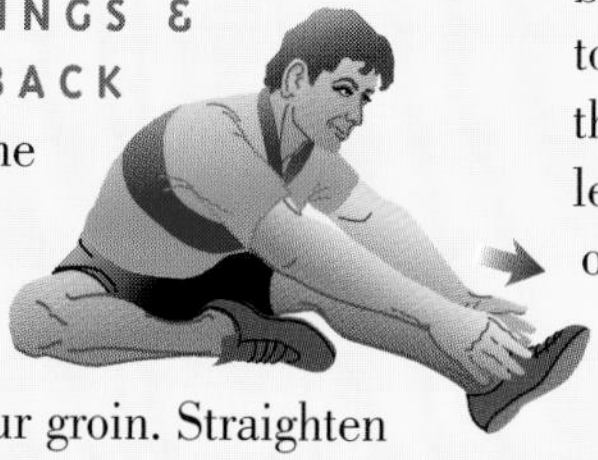

Sitting on the ground or floor, tuck your right foot into your groin. Straighten your left leg and reach as far forward as you can. Hold that position, then change to the other leg.

QUADRICEPS

Bracing yourself against a wall with your right hand, grab your right foot with your left hand and raise the leg as far as you can without cramping or pain. Now change to the other leg.

CALF & ACHILLES TENDON

Bracing yourself against a wall with one hand over the other, and your feet about 2 feet from the wall, bring your right leg forward and bend it at the knee. Moving your torso toward the wall, gently extend the calf and Achilles tendon of your left leg, keeping your left foot flat on the floor. Now change to the other leg.

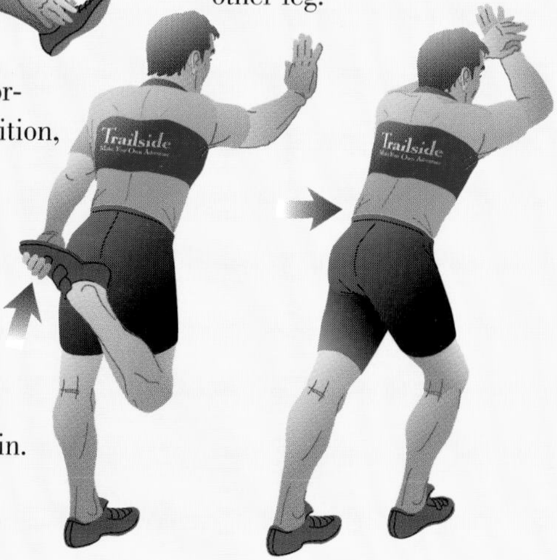

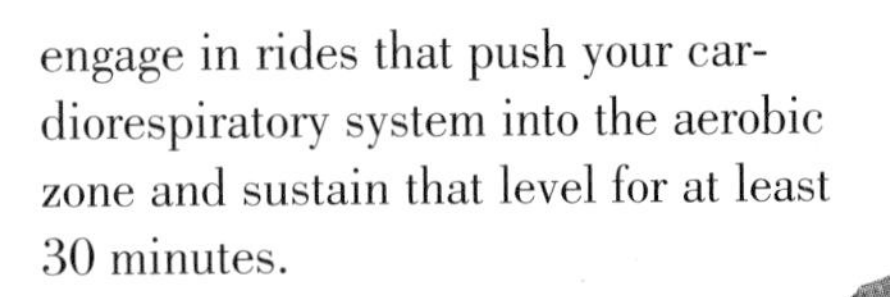

engage in rides that push your cardiorespiratory system into the aerobic zone and sustain that level for at least 30 minutes.

ENERGY BARS

How quickly the recreational world has become inundated with "energy" bars—quick fuel replenishment for backpackers, cyclists, runners, cross-country skiers, and others. Energy bars raise three questions: are they good nutrition, are they better than other forms of food, and are they worth the price?

The answer to the first question is yes and no. Loaded with simple carbohydrates, energy bars are great on-the-go fuel replenishment. They're quickly ingested so that their fuel can be quickly used. But they don't have much place in your regular diet, just as any food high in sugars should be eaten sparingly. (Sports "drinks"—usually high in carbohydrates and/or electrolytes—are another way to replenish energy quickly and easily.)

The answer to the second question is also yes and no. Foods like bananas and cookies can be just as good fuel resuppliers. The advantage of energy bars is that they're virtually indestructible. While bananas wilt and cookies crumble, a truck could drive over an energy bar to little or no effect. Energy bars also have the advantage of being easy to manipulate—easier than, say, a bag of trail mix or GORP—an important consideration when you're trying to eat while in the saddle.

As for the last question, energy bars typically run between $1.50 and $2, while a banana costs about 15¢. Yes, they're pricey, but their indestructibility and ease of use may make the extra expense worthwhile.

Variety is the spice of any good riding program. Vary your daily distances, terrain, and surroundings by mixing up the routes you take.

VARIETY, THE SPICE OF RIDING. Perhaps the most critical feature of any good riding program is variation. Variation is critical for rounded physiological development, building up not only your aerobic but anaerobic capacity as well. Your muscle tissue is formed from two basic fibers: fast-twitch, with a greater anaerobic capacity for short burst, and slow-twitch, with a greater aerobic capacity. Ideally, you want to develop both muscle types, and good variety in your daily rides should do the trick.

Variation has important psychological benefits, too. Doing the same ride over and over again is dull and pointless, given the bike's remarkable versatility in being able to take on different types of roads and terrain. Repetition leads to boredom, and boredom leads to your bike ending up unused in your garage or closet.

Vary your daily distances; for a recreational riding program, distances of between 10 and 50 miles represent a good range. Vary your intensity levels. Ride as hard as you can as far as you can one day, then ride leisurely the next. Combine in the same ride hard and easy riding, in what competitive riders call "interval" training, which is a good way of flexing those fast-twitch muscles. Start by riding easily, then push yourself for a mile or so to anaerobic excess. Ease off for a while to recover, push again, and so on. Vary the gears you ride in, spinning low gears rapidly one day and hammering high gears another.

Vary the terrain you ride, alternating between the flats, rolling terrain, and long, steep hills. And never, ever forget to include in your package of variations the fun ride, the cycling version of going out for a stroll. Go for a ride with your kids, your spouse, or your lover. Forget about your cadence or your heart rate or your muscular-twitch ratio or any of that human engine stuff. *Forget about it.* Instead, enjoy the world around you; enjoy the company you're with. Take it easy and love life on two wheels every once in a while. That's an upbeat attitude that will carry over and help sustain you through more strenuous rides.

Find a pace within your aerobic zone that you feel comfortable with, and you might surprise yourself with how long and far you can ride.

DID YOU KNOW

The record for cycling around the world is approximately 80 minutes. Astronauts on the space shuttle Columbia pulled off the feat, taking turns on a stationary bike while orbiting Earth.

Pacing Yourself

Establishing a comfortable pace can be tricky business, especially when seeking maximum variety in your riding. Some cyclists, with deep pockets and a deep obsession for statistical feedback, rely on computerized heart-rate monitors to help maintain an aerobic pace. If you've got $100 to $250 of disposable income sitting around, a heart-rate monitor is a great device, but it isn't essential. You need, simply, to tune into your body's signals—your heart rate, muscle fatigue, breathing (easy or labored), and so on—and respond accordingly with a riding pace you can maintain for at least an hour.

For road riding, 12 to 15 mph is a good average-pace starting point—fast enough to get you into the aerobic zone, but not so fast as to be overtaxing. From there, work on increasing your pace as your physical condition improves. You'll probably find it easy at first to bump your pace up one or two miles an hour. But as you begin to enter the 16- to 20-mph zone, you'll

Rest is an important element of both the physical and the mental game of enjoyable, beneficial cycling.

find each incremental gain harder won. A pace above 20 mph represents a high level of performance achieved only after hundreds—perhaps thousands—of miles of dedicated road work. Don't expect a miraculous ascent to that level after only a few days of riding around the block.

If road pacing is tricky, establishing a constant mountain-biking pace borders on impossibility. The syncopated cadences dictated by rough up-and-down terrain can render heart beats per minute or miles an hour all but meaningless. Again, the key is to attune yourself to your body's signals. Search for a pace (however erratic it might be) at which your body tells you you're pushing yourself but not straining. Settle on a pace you can sustain for an hour or more—while still leaving room for plenty of the antic, athletic playfulness that is so much a part of mountain biking's essential fun.

Rest

When they *really* get into their exercising, some aerobic athletes become so obsessive as to forget about taking a break. Rest is a critical part of any sensible exercise program. It gives hard-worked muscle and lung tissue a chance to rejuvenate. Rest is also part of the mental game of cycling, relieving the dulling sense of regimentation and duty that can creep into any riding program. If you are successful in developing a riding program you can stick with, congratulations. Now for the easy part: make sure to work in days here and there in which you permit yourself to be indulgently, and guiltlessly, lazy.

THE CLEAN, MEAN, RIDING MACHINE

A bike is a contraption of dazzling mechanical complexity made to seem simple—an interface of hundreds of moving parts. The chain alone is made of more than 100 flexible links, each incorporating several moving parts. When any of that intricately interactive movement becomes impeded by grit, gunk, moisture, or improper adjustment, the bike ceases operating at full capacity.

Propelling a lamed machine obviously entails more effort on your part. Perhaps not so obvious, until it may be too late to do much about it, is that neglected maintenance can be dangerous. It would be an unhappy moment, for example, to discover on a long and steep descent that your brakes won't brake. The clean, mean, well-tuned machine enhances both performance and safety.

BASIC MAINTENANCE: WHO, WHEN, AND WHERE

Some maintenance is very easy and quickly executed, while some maintenance is laborious and requires special tools. How much maintenance you choose to take on yourself and how much you choose to delegate to your local bike shop is your call. But if you do decide to do all the work yourself, you'll need to bring yourself up to speed on maintenance minutiae, and this chapter, unfortunately, won't do that for you.

Getting Help

The information in this chapter is rudimentary, extending not much beyond the most basic upkeep and repair. Don't despair—a number of books, some exquisitely detailed, have been written on bicycle maintenance and repair. Several are listed in the "Sources & Resources" section at the end of this book. Also, don't be afraid to ask questions of mechanics at your local bike shop. If you play your cards right, your bike-shop buddies will be willing to lend not only advice but tools as well, at least for use on the premises.

The regularity of maintenance depends greatly on where, how hard, and how often you ride. A mountain bike exposed to lots of rough terrain, mud, and grit may require more regular maintenance than a road bike ridden only on smooth surfaces. (On the other hand, the mud-caked, gunked-up bike is regarded by some mountain bikers as an emblem of great honor, certifying hard-core participation.) The key is vigilance: keep an eye out, on a regular basis, for maintenance needs.

THE BASIC HOW-TOS

Tire Talk

Most bikes are equipped with "clincher" tires. An inner tube is encased in a tire with sidewalls held in place by flanges extending from the wheel rim. Pretty much all recreational riders, as well as many racers, use clinchers, and there is a 99 percent certainty that your wheels are clincher-clad. Only a few high-end racing bikes have "sew-up" or "tubular" tires, which are glued to the rim. Once the standard for road racing, tubulars are gradually becoming rarer and rarer, to be used now only by high-level road racers and a die-hard corps of tubular devotees.

CLEAN TREADS. The first rule of tire maintenance is: keep them clean. You

LEARNING ABOUT YOUR BIKE

A good way to become intimately acquainted with your bike is to take a basic maintenance class. In the late autumn and winter, when business slows down, many bike shops offer maintenance courses. If your favorite shop is not offering classes, tell them you'd like to take one. Often, if enough customers express interest in a class, a shop will organize one. Another place to check for basic maintenance classes is through a local university extension service or "mini-course" listing. Community colleges and technical schools also frequently hold bike-maintenance classes. And check in with your local bicycle club, as clubs sometimes hold maintenance clinics.

Periodically checking your brakes for cable tension and alignment can be a life-saver, especially before a steep descent on a mountain bike.

can do this while riding as well as at home. After riding across a particularly nasty patch of pavement, experienced road riders often reach down (with a gloved hand, please) while riding and hold a hand lightly against the moving tire tread. This can brush away loose gunk that has affixed itself to the tread—gunk that could otherwise become embedded and later cause a flat. But this is not a particularly thorough cleaning procedure, especially for deep-treaded tires. After a ride on gravel, shale, road shoulders in populated areas (infamous as high-frequency broken-glass and road gunk zones), or other iffy surfaces, a quick post-ride—or even mid-ride—tire check is a smart precautionary move. It may save you from a flat tire somewhere down the road.

AIR TIME. The second rule is: inflate them properly. Underinflated inner tubes can become pinched between the rim and the edge of the tire, and overinflated tires are susceptible to bursting. Underinflated tires can also

DID YOU KNOW

Graeme Obree, who in 1994 briefly held the world record for the distance covered in an hour, set his record on a self-designed bike that included parts from a washing machine.

Encourage your kids to learn basic repairs such as tire changing. They'll thank you when they have a blow-out far from home.

result in rims getting bent or out of true.

Fatter tires—those found on mountain bikes and most hybrids—can usually be inflated to about 70 pounds per square inch (psi). As a rule of thumb, the smoother the riding surface, the higher your tire pressure should be. For rougher or looser (that is, off-road) surfaces, you'll probably want to reduce pressure for a smoother ride and to increase traction. Yet you're only courting the flat-tire demons by reducing your tire pressure much below 30 psi. Road-bike tires should generally be inflated at between 70 and 100 psi.

Check with a bike-shop mechanic for the appropriate pressure range for your tires, and reinflate often. Bike tires lose air pressure quickly—much more quickly than car tires. You're better off using your own pump than relying on service-station air hoses, which are notoriously unreliable at higher air pressures. Floor-standing pumps with pressure gauges aren't especially expensive, costing between $20 and $40, and are well worth the investment.

When inflating tires, cup the head of the pump in your hand and extend your thumb over the tire tread to keep the pump's nozzle securely fixed over the valve.

FIXING FLATS. No matter how diligently you take care of your tires, somewhere in your riding life you'll get a flat. To be ready for that possibility, you should always bring along an extra inner tube, two or three tire irons, and a frame pump. An adept tire changer can be back riding within five

Repairing a Flat Tire: (1) With a tire iron, reach between the tire sidewall and the edge of the rim and gently lever the sidewall over the rim edge. (2) Repeat this process until about 6 inches of the tire sidewall are over the rim. (3) Using your repair kit, carefully patch the tube. Now, partially inflate the patched tube (4) before working it back into the rim to help keep it from being pinched.

minutes. Don't expect to achieve such lightning quickness on your first few tire changes, and you might want to practice the process, just to get the hang of it. On some dreadfully dull evening, when your life has no better divertissement to offer, pop off the front wheel and give it a go. It's not exactly high entertainment, but a practice run-through at home can go far in taking the hassles out of a tire change on the road.

HERE'S THE BASIC PROCEDURE:

1) Using the flat, unnotched side of one tire iron, reach down between the tire sidewall and the edge of the rim. Gently lever the sidewall over the rim edge, then secure the notched end of

A basic tool kit might include (from top left): spare inner tube, lubricant, duct tape, tube-patching kit, adjustable wrench, chain tool, crankarm wrench, Allen wrenches, and tire irons. A pump is, of course, another must.

the tire iron to a spoke. Repeat this process until about six inches of the tire sidewall are over the rim. Now—again, *gently,* so as not to damage the tire or a punctured tube that may be reparable—run a tire iron between the tire sidewall and the rim edge around the rim, until the sidewall is completely over the rim.

2) Remove the fully deflated tube, starting at the valve. You might have to remove a locknut that holds the valve in place above the rim surface.

3) Carefully inspect the tire inside and out for the cause of the flat. Remove any sharp object you find before inflating.

4) Partially inflate the replacement tube, until it begins to take on its round shape. This will make the new tube easier to install and will lessen the chance of the tube becoming pinched when the sidewall is repositioned inside the rim edge.

5) Starting with the valve, insert the new tube under the tire. Being sure that no part of the tube is exposed or getting pinched, pull the sidewall back up over the rim edge. Start on the opposite side of the wheel from the valve.

6) Before inflating the tire fully, manipulate the tire with your thumb and fingers, working all the way around the tire circumference to be sure the sidewall is in place and the tube isn't pinched. Inflate, and you're ready to roll again.

Spinning True

The wheel—the invention so often credited with elevating humans above savagery—rises to a level of miracle only when it is perfectly round. A perfectly round wheel—a wheel that follows a perfect circle on an even vertical plane when spun—is called a "true" wheel; a wheel that doesn't spin in a perfect circle is considered "out of true."

FOR TRUE TRUING, GET HELP. Truing a wheel yourself is not easy, and doing it *wrong* is worse than not doing it at all. Truing is a part of your regular maintenance program best left to an experienced mechanic at a bike shop. But

THE BASIC TOOL KIT

FOR THE ROAD:

Small flathead screwdriver
Set of hex or Allen wrenches
Tire irons
Tube-patching kit
Extra inner tube
Pump (small enough to fit on your frame)
Spoke wrench
Pocket knife

WHAT YOU NEED AT HOME:

Adjustable wrench or a set of fixed-span wrenches
Heavy adjustable wrench (mainly for stubborn cogset or freewheel removal)
Freewheel tool
Floor pump
Chain tool
Tube-patching kit
Cleaning solution
Solvent
Chain lubricant
Cable cutter
Tires

WHAT'S NICE TO HAVE AT HOME:

Third hand tool (for use when adjusting brakes)
Workstand
Cone wrenches (to work on wheel hubs)
Small replacement parts: bearings, brake pads, brake and gear cables, derailleur pulleys, spokes, and so on)

When using a spoke wrench, make no more than a quarter of a turn at a time. Tightening a spoke too much can result in a misshapen, perhaps unsafe wheel.

you can, by using a spoke wrench, make minor adjustments as needed, especially after an unpleasant encounter with some wheel-jarring obstacle such as a rock or pothole. Make sure, by the way, to get the right-sized wrench for turning your spoke nipples.

The best way to determine if a wheel is true is to spin it and use the brake pads as points of reference. If the rim appears to wobble or brushes against one brake pad, the wheel is out of true. Rough terrain, riding with a flat tire for any extended distance, or a crash are among the leading causes of tires going out of true.

THE SOUND OF A TRUE WHEEL. Use a spoke wrench to tighten loose spokes, turning no more than a quarter of a turn at a time—spokes too tight are as bad as spokes too loose. Spin the wheel and run a finger across the spokes. You should hear a mono-tonal harmony, with all spokes ringing out the same key. A lower tone indicates that a spoke may be loose. If there still seems to be a wobble in the wheel, take it to a bike shop as soon as possible for an expert truing job.

Maintaining the Drivetrain

Pedals don't require much maintenance. You should, however, clear away any gunk that could get kicked into the chain or gear rings or that could clog up your cleats, if your bike

ADJUSTING THE QUICK RELEASE

The quick release lever is a neat mechanism that allows you to remove and re-install your wheels with the flick of a lever; no wrenches or other tools are needed. But for all that they are convenient, failure to properly install and adjust wheels equipped with quick release levers can cause wheels to come off mid-ride, with an accident the probable result, and serious injury a real possibility. A surprising number of cyclists do not tighten the quick release nut properly. Here's how it's done.

Be sure to operate the quick release lever by hand only. Never use any other tool such as a hammer to tighten the lever, as it could cause damage.

ATTACHING THE WHEEL

1. Move the quick release lever to the OPEN position and set the wheel so it firmly touches the interior of the fork end.

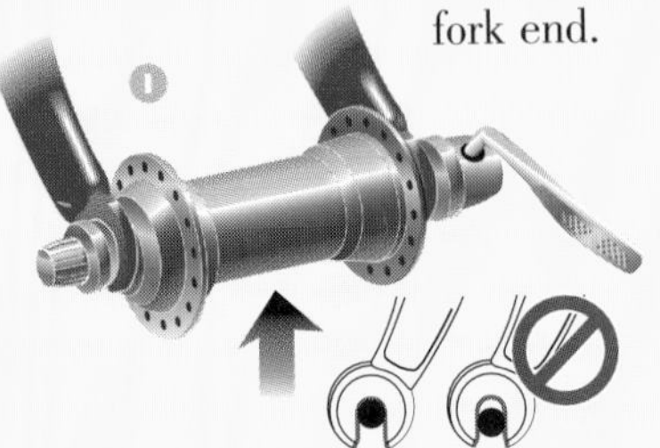

2. Move the quick-release lever to a position perpendicular to the bicycle frame (halfway between the opened and closed positions). Using your hand, turn the adjusting nut clockwise until it can no longer be turned.

3. Turn the lever to the CLOSED position. The lever should be pointed toward the rear of the bike and positioned along the fork blade. Be sure to

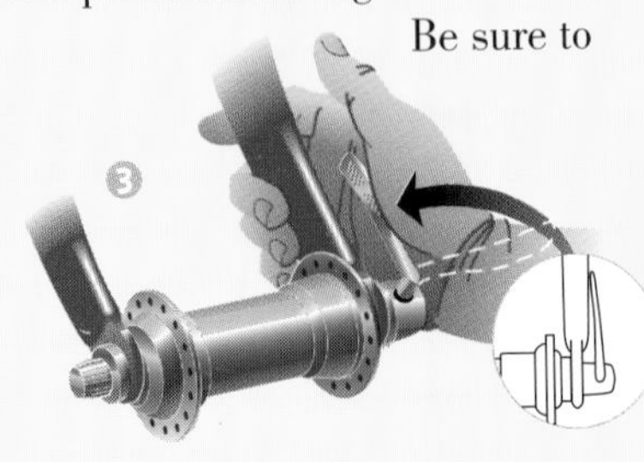

is equipped with them.

QUICK CLEANING. Your chain, chain rings, and cogset or freewheel do call for frequent and regular maintenance. They should be cleaned and re-lubed often, especially the chain, with its hundreds of tiny crannies eager to harbor insidious grime. This can be messy business, and you might want to wear old clothes and use rubber gloves to protect your hands against the grime and harsh solvents.

---

push the lever all the way to the closed position.

CAUTION: You cannot fasten the front wheel by twisting the quick release lever.

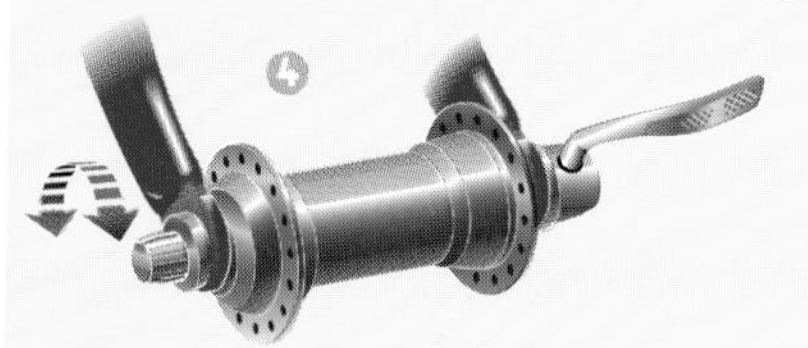

4 If the quick release lever can be easily pushed to the closed position, its clamping strength is insufficient. Return the lever to a position halfway between opened and closed (with the lever perpendicular to the bike frame), and again turn the adjusting nut clockwise to increase clamping strength. Push the quick release lever back to the closed position.

If the nut is so tight that the quick release lever cannot be pushed to the closed position, return it to the halfway position and turn the adjusting nut counter-clockwise to reduce the clamping strength.

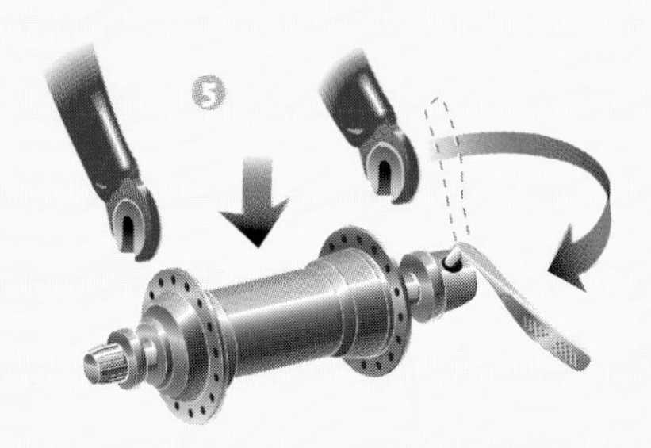

REMOVING THE WHEEL

5 Move the quick release lever to the open position. This will release the wheel, and it can be removed. There is no need to move the adjusting nut when removing the wheel.

BEFORE YOU RIDE

- Check your quick release, making sure the lever is pushed fully to the closed position.
- Lift up your bike so the front wheel is off the ground and give the top of the tire a sharp downward blow. The wheel should not come off or feel loose. This is only a quick check, and does not guarantee that the quick release lever has received adequate tightening torque. If uncertain, repeat the tightening process.

You can use a synthetic bike oil (not WD-40 or 3-in-1 oil). To do your cleaning, you'll need a small brush and a couple of old rags. (An old toothbrush will do.) For simple and regular riding (as in after every 100 to 200 miles), simply run a clean rag around the chain, working the links of the chain between your fingers to remove the crud. Then apply the lubricant, *very sparingly,* to the inner portion of the chain links, using the clean rag to wipe off the excess.

GO LIGHTLY. Using too much lubricant—or a lubricant that is too heavy—is like applying a gunk magnet to your chain. It won't take more than a few miles of riding before an overly lubricated chain has sucked up enough road grit to become gummy or stiff. Use less lubricant than you think you should; if necessary, you can always apply more. (If you hear your chain squeaking, you need to lube.)

When lubing your chain, apply lubricant sparingly. Too much lubricant will attract road (or trail) grit, leading quickly to a gummy, inflexible chain.

Cleaning the cogset or freewheel and front chainrings is something you might not want to do with every chain cleaning; doing it during every second or third chain cleaning is probably sufficient. Your small brush—a device to sneak in between the gear teeth—is the tool of choice here.

Deep Cleaning

At some point—perhaps once or twice a season, depending on how often you ride—it's a good idea to disassemble the drive train completely for a thorough cleaning. A thorough cleaning does, however, require some mechanical expertise, so don't jump into the procedure unless you're sure of what you are doing. You will need to "cut" and remove the chain with a chain tool and remove gear rings. If you are unsure of how to do this properly—or how to reassemble your drive train—have the first few deep cleanings done at a local bike shop.

Don't be afraid to ask the shop mechanic questions, especially on the chain-cutting procedure. Then, when you feel confident to disassemble the

Who says you have to have a clean riding machine? For some riders a dirty bike is more a badge of honor than a performance impediment.

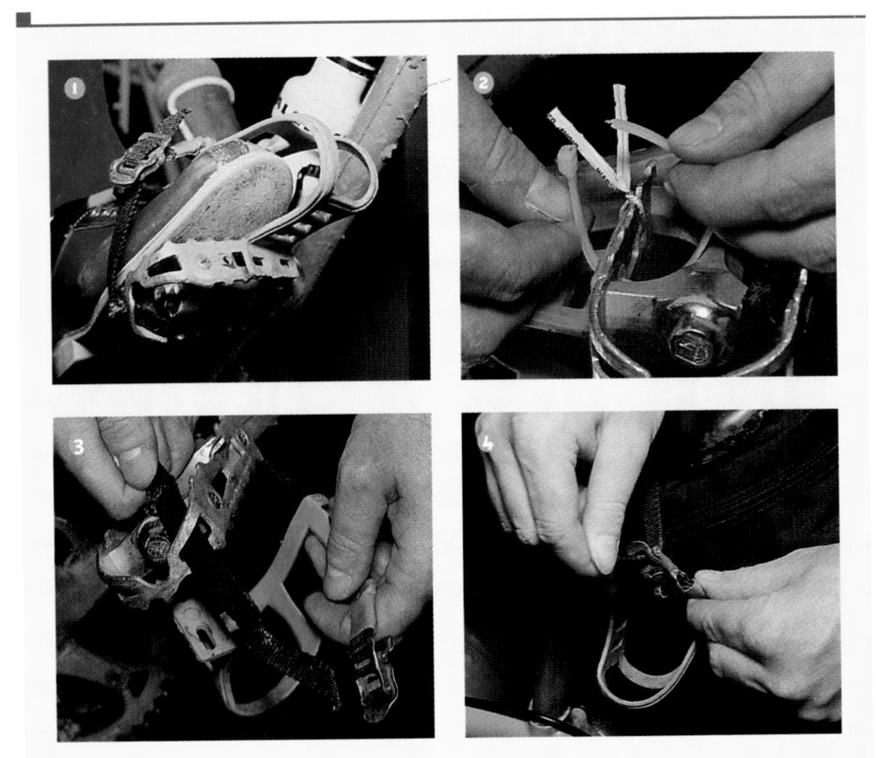

GEAR TALK

ON-THE-TRAIL REPAIR: MISSING TOE CLIP BOLTS

The point here is to be resourceful and imaginative in the face of mechanical failures large and small when you're out on the trail far from any town, much less bike repair shop. A toe clip is a simple enough device, but when you lose not just one bolt, but the second one as well (1), it's time for some ingenuity. Lots of things will do the trick in a pinch, including plastic bag ties (2), a shoe lace, cord from a windbreaker waist or hood cinch, or duct tape. Or snitch one of the two bolts off your other toe clip.

Nothing with which to make the repair? Then remove the entire clip, strap and all (3). Trying to ride with the leather strap alone is a bad idea, since it's too difficult to get in and out of it without the metal clip. Secure the clip under your saddle (4) to get it home. Once there, make sure to tighten the bolts on the other toe clip when you reattach the one that fell off. And check the entire bike for loose fittings.

drivetrain components on your own, you'll have a clearer sense of how to proceed. You also would do well to consult one of several books on bicycle repair (see "Sources & Resources" at the back of this book).

Adjusting the Derailleurs

The derailleurs should keep your chain restricted to within the appropriate shifting range. A chain that gets dumped into your spokes or drops off of the front chain rings is a hazard most often caused by a maladjusted derailleur. With index shifters—an increasingly common feature on new bikes—this is not the issue it is with conventional friction shifting.

SURE SHIFTING. Look for two small "stop" screws on both your front and your rear derailleur. These screws limit the shifting range: one limits how far you can shift to the inside, the other limits how far you can shift toward the outside. Loosening the screws increases the shifting range; tightening them decreases the range. To adjust the derailleurs properly, run through the complete range of gears, front and back. Make special note of how smoothly the chain travels in the highest and lowest gears. Is there a grinding sound? Does the chain scrape against the front derailleur? If so, turn the appropriate adjustment screw a quarter turn at a time, moving the derailleur ever so slightly and allowing the chain to line up properly with the gear wheels. Increasing the range too much can result in your chain jumping off the chain rings. Constricting the range too much will mean you won't be able to use all your gears.

Top: A small hand-adjustment screw, where the cable from the shifter meets the derailleur, can be tightened to pick up slack in the cable. Bottom: Two small screws in the rear derailleur are "stop" screws that limit your shifting range. Proper adjustment prevents over-shifting and the "dumping" of the chain off the highest or lowest gear.

KEEPING CABLES TIGHT. Derailleur cables stretch and slip, and from time to time you might feel it necessary to cinch up the cable tension. Cable stretch or slippage shouldn't affect

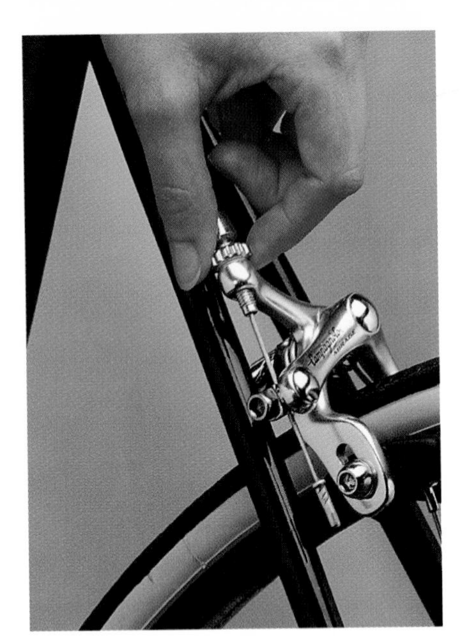

A hand adjustment screw on the brakes allows you to increase, or lessen, cable tension when necessary for safer, more accurate braking.

your overall gear range; that's what the stop screws are for. Still, cables should be taut to maintain smooth, accurate shifting. And if your bike has index shifters, loose cables can throw off the indexing, dumping the chain between gears or on the wrong gear ring when a shift is executed. If you do find the need to cinch up your cables, make sure to readjust the derailleur settings, if necessary, before riding.

Better Braking

Although brakes usually don't require much maintenance, they should be checked regularly (perhaps before every ride); they are your principal safety devices. As such, you should always consult your bike mechanic if you are the least unsure about performing the following adjustments. Focus on three things: alignment, cable tension, and brake pads.

PROPER ALIGNMENT. The pads should be aligned evenly over the rims (not the tires). If the alignment is off, use a socket wrench to loosen the nut holding the pad to the brake arm, correct the alignment, and retighten the nut. If your brakes squeal, they may need to be "toed in," which is an adjustment a bicycle mechanic can make in seconds. (Toeing in the brake pads means the front of the pad will touch the rim slightly before the rear of the pad, eliminating that squealing noise.)

The brake cables should be taut enough so that you begin to feel the application of brake pressure after depressing the brake levers only an inch or so. Most brakes have a small adjustment screw for minor tightening adjustments. This is easy work; no tools—other than a thumb and a finger—are needed.

PAD REPLACEMENT. Brake pads, depending on the kind of riding you do, should last for at least two years of regular riding. But check periodically for wear, especially *uneven* wear. If one pad is more worn down than the other, you may have to have your brakes recentered over the wheel—a job done within seconds by a competent bike mechanic.

Keeping Bearings Straight

In the genesis of cycling, first there were wheels, then there were bearings. If it weren't for the sixty or so bearings packed into the wheel hubs and the

A small tool kit, easily secured under your saddle or in a handlebar pack, can make on-the-fly repairs quick and simple.

bottom bracket of a bike, there simply wouldn't be a bike. You would exhaust yourself battling against the friction of metal against metal.

Fortunately, bearings on most new bikes require virtually no maintenance. Most new bikes are equipped with hubs and bottom brackets with bearings sealed securely from noxious grime or moisture. Sealed "cartridge" bottom brackets and sealed hubs are terrific news for most cyclists. The only problem is that if there is a problem, your only recourse is to replace the malfunctioning hub or bottom bracket. Nevertheless, the good news is that sealed-bearing bottom brackets and hubs tend to hold up remarkably well, usually for several years of regular riding.

Older bikes may well have unsealed bearings, in which case they'll need to be cleaned and repacked periodically, perhaps every 3,000 miles or so. This is probably a job best performed by an experienced mechanic, but if you feel inclined to do it yourself, consult a detailed maintenance book on the procedure, and work fastidiously. Loose bearings have a diabolical way of escaping, and poorly repacked bearings can severely damage your bike.

Replacing Parts

Well-maintained bike parts can last a remarkably long time. In most cases, you'll probably find yourself buying parts to upgrade your bike, rather than to replace worn parts. But when you do decide a part needs replacing, be sure you know your bike's specifications. Wheel sizes differ, screw threading differs, chain widths differ, and so on. You don't want to spend, say, $40 on a new cogset or freewheel only to find that it doesn't fit on your rear hub.

TIRES. Tubes and tires are the parts that require the most frequent replacement. Don't worry about short, worn patches on your tire treads; these can develop even on a new tire after a sudden, skidding stop. Instead, examine your treads for overall wear and for significant cuts and tears. There is no reasonable timetable for tire replacement: 1,000 miles on harsh surfaces can trash a tire that might last ten times as long on smoother surfaces.

THE CHAIN. You'll probably want to replace your chain every 3,000 to 4,000 miles. Chains rust, corrode, stretch, get bent out of shape, develop stiff links, and just plain wear out from the grind they're put through. Chain replacement isn't essential, because old chains rarely break or lock up completely. But when you can by a new chain for as little as $6, why not do it when it can dramatically improve the smoothness of your ride? Just make sure to count the number of links in your old chain and, using a chain tool, cut your new chain down to the same length.

THE COGSET OR FREEWHEEL. Bike mechanics often recommend replacing the cogset or freewheel whenever you replace the chain. The pattern of wear on the cog teeth, produced by the old chain, might not mesh smoothly with the new chain, leading to skipping and gear-shifting problems. But a new cogset or freewheel isn't always necessary; the best thing to do is to stick with your existing cogset or freewheel with the new chain for the first few rides. If the two mesh smoothly, a new cogset or freewheel is an investment you can hold off on making.

After about 5,000 miles, it's not a bad idea to have a shop replace your brake and shifting cables. Old cables aren't likely to break, but they do rust,

GEAR TALK

EXTRA COGSETS OR FREEWHEELS

Cyclists who ride a wide range of terrain often have more than one cogset or freewheel. They'll have one with big cogwheels for ease of climbing and another with smaller cogwheels for mostly flat riding. If you have a freewheel tool, having an extra cogset or freewheel is an option you might want to consider. An extra one costs between $15 and $50.

stretch, slip, and get gummed up in their casings. Make sure that when you do replace the cables, the brakes and gear shift levers are properly adjusted. They will probably stretch or slip within the first 100 miles or so of riding, so be sure to readjust them if necessary.

THE BIKE SHOP AS RESOURCE

When shopping for a bike, the best bike shop is the one that gives you good service and a good deal. But a bike shop can mean a lot more in your cycling life than a good initial fit and a few dollars saved. A good bike shop can be your most valuable single resource, comparable to a pro shop for golfers. It is a place not only to buy gear but also to repair gear and to seek advice and information on a wide variety of topics.

A reliable local bike shop can become your most valuable single resource.

For starters, the shop you buy from should have an "aftercare" program. Good shops usually offer thirty-day checkups as part of a sales package; return to the store in thirty days to make sure the cables haven't stretched, the brakes are still aligned, the gears shift properly, and all things are in crisp working order. Some shops offer a free tune-up within the first year of buying a new bike.

Thereafter, don't be afraid to make use of the shop's maintenance expertise. If you can't figure out which screw fits in which hole, what to do about the squeak in your brakes, how to realign a faulty derailleur, or the solution to any other maintenance mystery, ask the shop mechanics. If you're a solid citizen and a regular customer, you may even be lent tools or be allowed to make use of the shop's work stands.

Looking for a route to ride? When visiting an unfamiliar area with his bike on board, Alan Coté, who writes for many cycling publications, including *MTB* and *Velo-News,* makes a beeline for a local bike shop. "People who work in bike shops are usually riders who know where the best rides are," says Coté. Bike shops are also a likely place to find local maps and guidebooks on rides.

Looking for people to ride with, either casually or competitively? Some shops have ride listings, and any good shop should be able to direct you to a local bike club. Special cycling events, charity rides, local races—a bike shop is probably the best place to find out about them.

For information on bike shops in your area—or an area you plan to visit—contact the National Bicycle Dealers Association, listed in the "Sources & Resources" section at the end of this book.

The only limits to a clean, mean riding machine are your own, and they will become fewer and fewer the more you ride.

10 THE TAO OF TWO WHEELS

Before brushing that aside as some rallying cry for the cause of aerobic evangelism, give it some thought. Unlike many other forms of exercise, cycling can be integrated into your daily life with minimal lifestyle change or personal sacrifice.

True enough, time is often the enemy of many would-be cyclists trying to establish a regular riding regimen. Riding in excess of, say, 100 miles a week calls for a weekly commitment of six hours or more—six-plus hours that might not be available in a life in which work, family, and such mundane obligations as house cleaning, tax paying, and lawn mowing can consume "free time." Yet unlike activities such as golf, skiing, tennis, and even running, cycling can entwine itself with relative ease in the web of daily activities.

Riding a bike can be a means of getting to and from work, a means of coping with daily errands and chores, a means of sharing time with friends and family, a means of *competing* with family and friends. It is obviously a means of getting in shape and staying fit, which—given the fact that you are reading this book—presumably ranks high among your personal priorities. And it is a means that, very likely, is available to you as you read this sentence, with a bike sitting somewhere nearby among your stash of playthings.

Part of the fun of cycling in a group is planning a day's ride together.

If you're serious about your riding, you'll want to—and will have to—set aside a few hours for serious aerobic grunt work. But all your riding needn't be like that. Continue doing all the things you normally do, only start doing some of those things on a bike: bringing cycling into your life can be as simple as that. And you can do so in at least three ways: communing with others, commuting to and from work, and competing.

COMMUNING

Cycling is one of the most engagingly sociable, everybody-into-the-pool forms of recreation known to man. Cycling is not like golf, pickup basketball, touch football, tennis, or racquetball—sports that enisle participants in the exclusive company of a cadre of fellow athletes. Quite to the contrary. Riding a bike is as egalitarian a form of exercise as there is.

FOR ALL AGES. . . Every year, people in their sixties and seventies join organized tours covering more than 3,500 miles from coast to coast; thus cycling, Q.E.D., is not a sport in which senior citizenship enforces retirement from active duty. At the other end of the age spectrum, younger kids, riding in rumble seats on rear-mounted racks or towed in trailers, can safely be brought on board. The Adventure Cycling Association reports that kids under a year old have accompanied their parents on coast-to-coast rides. Most kids are ready to do their own pedaling at four or five and participate in short family rides—if not necessarily a transcontinental tour—by the time they're seven.

GEAR TALK

BIKES FOR KIDS

How do you go about bringing your kids up the cycling ladder? Tim Blumenthal, executive director of the International Mountain Biking Association and father of two, suggests the following progression:

- Around 3 years old—This is the "big-wheeler" phase, when kids simply get the feel for pedaling and being around wheels. Big-wheelers are those plastic tricycles available for under $50 at department stores. They're low to the ground so that kids can't hurt themselves seriously in a fall. Stick to driveways, sidewalks, and traffic-free parking areas. And before you involve your kids in any kind of riding, be sure to get them helmets.
- 5 to 7 years old—This is "two-wheeler time," says Blumenthal, when kids should be ready to step up to real bicycling. A single-geared bike with coaster brakes—usually available for $80 or less—is the ideal machine. For first-time riding, find a very smooth paved surface, preferably with a very gentle downhill leading to a very gentle uphill. That way, your child can build momentum without having to worry much about pedaling and stop without having to worry about braking. Shopping-mall parking lots on Sunday mornings are great first-time rider zones. Start with the saddle low, so that the feet can touch the ground easily.
- 8 to 11 years old—This is "the really exciting stage," says Blumenthal, when kids are ready for joining you on real rides. Again, a single-geared, coaster-braking bike should work just fine. Be sure to pick relatively easy terrain, with minimal elevation changes.
- 12 to 14 years old—This is Blumenthal's "age of enlightenment," when kids "really start getting into it." It's time to look at multigeared mountain bikes, and you should be able to find something able to stand up to rigorous riding for under $250. Buy at a bike shop rather than a department store, where assembly of more complicated bikes can be suspect.
- 14 and up—Your child, in cycling years, is basically an adult now, but Blumenthal recommends sticking with kids' bikes as long as possible. Kids' mountain bikes are basically adult bikes, at a fraction of the cost.

. . . AND BOTH GENDERS. Gender equality is another of cycling's attractive qualities. In the breakdown of adult cyclists, the Bicycle Institute of America reports that women represent a larger share (55 percent) of the cycling population than men. One shudders to think of how such sports as pickup basketball and touch football stack up against that gender equation.

The Price Is Right

And even in the age of the $3,000 titanium frame, cycling needn't exclude those of limited financial wherewithal. According to the Worldwatch Institute, only 10 percent of the *world's* population has the means to buy a car, while 80 percent can afford a bike. That's the world's population—presumably, in the relatively affluent United States, the percentage of those able to afford a bike is even higher. Once you've got a bike, you don't have to pay for greens fees, lift tickets, court time, or health-club memberships. You don't have to shell out mega-bucks to travel to special cycling resorts, as is often the case for skiing or golf. All you have to do is walk out the door, put on your helmet, get on, and start pedaling.

So if your weekend schedule typically involves sitting around the house with family or friends, why not do that sitting around on the seat of a bike instead? Consider it mobile, rather than sedentary, socializing. Another way to be socially mobile, so to speak, is to join a local bike club—a way of expanding your personal fellowship of riders. The organizing of group rides—competitive rides, training rides, fun rides—is the raison d'être of most clubs, and many go a step further, spearheading social and political activities.

Go on—get back on your bike and recapture the spirit of childhood!

There's no gender gap among cyclists. In fact, in America, women represent a larger share (55 percent) of the cycling population than men.

DID YOU KNOW

The American Academy of Pediatrics Committee on Sports Medicine and Fitness recommends that you take it easy when taking kids under six years old along on your cycling jaunts. Short attention span and under-developed motor skills, the Committee reports, greatly increase the chances of an accident. Take it slow, go on short rides, stop often, and include fun places to stop: These are among the Committee's suggestions for making rides with kids safer and more fun.

FINDING FELLOW RIDERS. The League of American Bicyclists, a national advocacy organization for cyclists, reports that among its member organizations are 450 active bike clubs in the United States. The Adventure Cycling Association lists close to 150 clubs in *The Cyclists' Yellow Pages,* while the International Mountain Biking Association includes more than 200 member clubs. Adventure Cycling, IMBA, or the LAB (see Sources & Resources) should be able to help track down an active club in your area, and these numbers certainly don't represent all U.S. bike clubs.

JOINING A CLUB RIDE. Some clubs require you to be a member in order to join a ride, others don't. In some cases, you might be charged a minimal fee as a nonmember to participate in a ride or asked to sign an insurance waiver. Yet as Tim Rahto, information specialist for the LAB points out, "Most clubs welcome nonmembers on rides. It's a way to help increase membership." Often, group rides arise through the personal initiative of a club member simply looking for the company of other riders on his

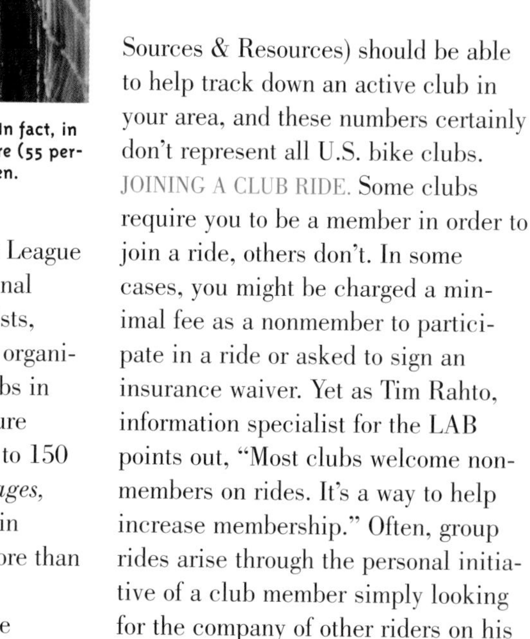

Bicycle tour boarding a ferry, Seattle, Washington. Whether joining up with a local bike club ride or signing on with a tour operator, cycling presents many opportunities for sharing the adventure.

or her favorite ride.

Clubs with ride listings usually do a pretty good job of ranking the difficulty of each ride according to its length and expected average speed. In many cases, options—to ride longer or shorter routes, or at faster or slower paces—are offered. But if you're unsure of your fitness or ability, start with the easiest rides and work your way up. In some cases, rides may be restricted to certain types of riders—racers in training, older riders, families, and so on. Also the number of riders, primarily for safety reasons, might be limited. In other words, it's a wise idea to call the club about a ride beforehand, rather than simply showing up at the designated starting point and time.

Large-Scale Communing

Bike clubs, community organizations, and charities often organize and sponsor rides or festivals that draw hundreds—even thousands—of participants. Often such rides are organized to raise money for worthy causes, although that's not always the case. Bike shops, the sports pages of the local newspaper, bike clubs, and chambers of commerce are good sources of information on major cycling events in your area. For an idea of what to expect, the following is a sampling of well-established social cycling events in the United States.

ASSAULT ON MOUNT MITCHELL, NORTH CAROLINA. Every year—in late May or early June—more than 1,500 riders decide that a 102-mile ride finishing with a 5,000-foot vertical climb of Mount Mitchell (highest east of the Rockies) is an irresistibly enchanting idea. For information, contact the Spartanburg Freewheelers, Box 6161, Spartanburg, SC 29304; 803-578-3171.

THE DAVIS DOUBLE CENTURY. If you're aching to find out if you're capable of riding 200 miles in one sitting, check out this ride, held the third weekend in May in Davis, California. The hard-core riders finish in under 10 hours; normal folks may take twice that time. For information, contact the Davis Bicycle Club, 610 3rd St., Davis, CA 95616; 916-756-3540.

FAT TIRE BIKE WEEK IN CRESTED BUTTE, COLORADO. Among the hallowed places in the development of mountain biking, Crested Butte ranks just behind Marin County. This festival, held in July, has thus become one of mountain biking's annual get-togethers, featuring races, fun rides, and silliness, all at lung-busting high altitude. For information, contact Fat Tire Bike Week, Box 782, Crested Butte, CO 81224; 303-349-6817.

Large-scale communing among cyclists means taking time out to rest as well as ride.

RAGBRAI (REGISTER'S ANNUAL GREAT BICYCLE RIDE ACROSS IOWA). Held at the end of July, this full-week event, covering more than 500 miles, might be a race for a hard-core few driven by competitive impulses. But for thousands of other participants, it's a communal happening, a family affair. The field is limited, so you'll have to sign up months in advance. For information, contact RAGBRAI, Box 622, Des Moines, IA 50303; 515-284-8282.

THE TOUR OF THE SCIOTO RIVER VALLEY, OHIO. This 210-mile, two-day ride is into its fourth decade—one of the most famous nonracing rides in the United States. Between 3,000 and 4,000 riders show up every year. For information, contact TOSRV, Box 14384, Columbus, OH 43214; 614-447-1006.

THE WEST VIRGINIA FAT TIRE FESTIVAL, WEST VIRGINIA. West Virginia has emerged as the East Coast's mountain-biking hot spot. Every June, the fat tire crowd gathers for a week of rides,

Thailand, just one of the many exotic foreign lands cyclists can explore. This is a Backroads tour.

clinics, bluegrass music, and other forms of fun and games. For information, contact the Elk River Touring Center, Hwy. 219, Slatyfork, WV 26291; 304-572-3771.

COMMUTING

Commuting is an American way of life, and commuting by car an American addiction. It is probably fair to speculate that most car commuters could switch to bike commuting with minimal change in their lifestyles. Consider a typical, five-mile commuting scenario: a car averaging 30 mph would make that trip in 10 minutes. Yet throw in the likelihood of traffic congestion, and the trip might well take considerably longer. A cyclist traveling 12 mph would make the same trip in 25 minutes, rarely having to worry about traffic jams. A few more minutes each morning and evening—not much.

The Benefits of Bike Commuting

One needn't speculate about the benefits of making the switch to commuting by bike. According to figures from the Colorado Department of Transportation's Bicycle Program, a person riding regularly to work—five miles each way—would save 130 gallons of gas a year. That person would also spare the environment 297 pounds of carbon monoxide, not to mention other noxious effluvia sent airborne by automotive exhaust. And, obviously enough, that person would be physically more fit than the person commuting by car. Bicycle commuting makes good sense.

Unfortunately, that good sense has yet to establish a firm foothold on the American commuting scene. Although the bicycle is commonly used as a means of transportation in Asian and European cities, bicycle trips represent less than 3 percent of all trips made in U.S. cities. In something of an irony from a cyclist's perspective, the city of Shanghai recently considered an ordinance banning bikes from the downtown district during rush hour because cars couldn't get through the swarms of cyclists. It's a reasonable surmise that such a problem is unlikely to arise in any U.S. city in the near future.

A Londoner on the way to work under his own steam. Common as a means of commuting in European cities, the bicycle makes up less than 3 percent of all trips made in U.S. cities.

Most Americans are apparently quite eager to see more done to make life easier for cyclists. In a recent Harris poll, 60 percent of all Americans indicated they'd like to see more government funds devoted to making the transportation system more bicycle and pedestrian friendly. In the same poll, half of America's adult cyclists said they would commute to work or school by bike at least some of the time if they felt it were safe to do so.

Helping Hand for Commuters

Government efforts on behalf of cyclists vary dramatically from city to city, region to region, and state to state. For example, *Bicycling* magazine not long ago rated Seattle, Missoula (Montana), Eugene (Oregon), and Washington, D.C., at the top of its list of best cycling cities in the country. It cited city governments for, among other things, developing bike paths and lanes, requiring office-building developers to include showers for cyclists and runners, and installing bike-friendly sewer grates. The League of American Bicyclists, in a survey a few years ago of U.S. states, praised the pro-cycling efforts of Oregon and Ohio.

But the LAB also ranked Missouri, Montana, and Nebraska at the bottom of its list. Not all regions and communities have done much to make life better for riders. But as LAB offi-

DID YOU KNOW

Contrary to a commonly held conception, racers don't shave their legs to be more aerodynamic. They do it to lessen the effects of "road rash"—scraped and cut skin from a fall. (Hair heightens the friction between road and legs in a crash—resulting in nastier rashes—inhibits treatment, and increases the chance of infection.) Also, shaved legs are easier to massage, a vital part of recovery after a long ride. And finally, many racers, though they rarely admit it, like the idea that shaving shows off their well-toned leg muscles.

cials point out, lack of organized effort, rather than an entrenched public resistance, has been the prime factor in holding back many communities from creating more bike-friendly environments. In other words, local governments and private companies are perfectly amenable to the idea of bicycle commuting, but they haven't a clue about what to do about it. That's where you, the prospective two-wheeling commuter, can come in.

Local transportation departments, cycling advocacy groups, and private companies need assistance. They need advice, suggestions, volunteer manpower—anything to set the wheels in motion, so to speak. Bike lanes, bike parking facilities, and showers and changing areas in office buildings are not difficult ideas to implement, but someone must take the lead. Working with local bike clubs or organizations is one way to get such ideas across to governmental bodies; organizing an "alternative commuter" group at your workplace is another way of going about it. If you're interested in riding your bike to and from work but are put off by the potential hassles involved, a little activism can go far in clearing up those hassles.

COMPETING

Given the high all-round fitness quotient cycling earns from the President's Council on Physical Fitness (see Chapter 8), riding is an excellent way of shaping up for many sports you might engage in. But it's obviously best as a conditioner for the sport you might not have given much thought to—bike racing.

To be sure, competitive cycling is not for everyone. As a popular form of communal competition, bike racing certainly lags behind such activities as running and softball. Probably its main drawback—other than equipment expenses, which can mount rapidly as you climb the competitive ladder—is its inherent risk. Serious accidents that require hospitalization don't happen often, but crashes resulting in bruises and lost skin are not uncommon. That said, bike racing can be scintillatingly fun stuff—challenging, exciting and, as you'd expect of anything cycling-related, broadly inclusive.

Racing through History

Interestingly enough, bike racing's traditions in American sporting life run far deeper than many people might expect. At the turn of the century, bicycle racing as a spectator sport was big stuff in America, bigger than baseball or football. In the early 1900s, six-day races—in which teams of riders rode around a bike track, or velodrome, for six consecutive days—would draw standing-room-only crowds to such famous arenas as Madison Square Garden in New York. It was bike racing that produced perhaps the first, widely respected black-American sports hero—Marshall "Major" Taylor (1878–1932), the dominant rider of his era.

As other sports grew, interest in bicycle racing waned, to the point where, twenty years ago, there were fewer than 20,000 licensed racers in the United States. But in recent years, helped along by the surge of interest in mountain biking, bike racing has

Citizens' races are rarely more than 10 miles. The point is to have fun with fellow cyclists.

experienced something of a renaissance. Today, according to the Bicycle Institute of America, there are approximately 400,000 Americans who race. That might be optimistic, but there are still close to 100,000 racers licensed by the U.S. Cycling Federation (USCF), the governing body of road racing, and the National Off-Road Bicycling Association (NORBA), the governing body of mountain-bike racing. A number of elite U.S. riders, both road racers and mountain bikers, are now making a healthy living as professionals—a fact barely imaginable just 15 years ago.

Getting Started

To get into racing—to *enjoy* racing—you hardly have to be driven by professional ambition, have limitless aerobic potential, or feel compelled to devote several hundred miles a week to training. Anyone with a helmet and a safe bike (well-maintained brakes and wheels, firmly attached handlebars) can compete in "citizens'" road races, while at many mountain-bike events you can buy a one-day racing license on the spot in order to enter beginner races.

CITIZENS' RACING. Citizens' and beginner races are often staged in conjunction with, or as preludes to, competitions for more advanced racers. In fact, one of the neat aspects of bike racing—like most road-running races—is that the world's finest competitors often compete at the same events, and on the same courses, as absolute novices.

Distances for citizens' or beginner races are rarely more than 10 miles. Often the first mile or two of a race is ridden at a moderate, controlled pace, allowing inexperienced racers to get used to riding in a tight pack. Sometimes an experienced racer or race organizer will ride along to explain race etiquette and safety. The idea is to have fun and to get a feel for the thrill and speed of racing. Thereafter, if you're sufficiently turned on by competitive riding, you can apply to the USCF or NORBA for an annual license to enter higher-level races. For insurance reasons (in case of an accident), you're best off sticking with USCF- or NORBA-sanctioned events.

RACING—WITHOUT COMPETING. Like organized fun rides, races are something parents and kids can both participate in. Races are often divided into age and ability groupings, a way of broadening the participation level. And bike clubs that organize regular races are almost always looking for help with course monitoring, timekeeping, and other race-support duties. So if your kids want to race but you don't (or vice versa), there are still noncompetitive ways to become involved in the racing scene. It's all about participation and inclusion—the tao of cycling in a nutshell.

SOURCES & RESOURCES

After reading this book you may be ready to grab your bike—or head for the nearest bike store to buy a new one—and rekindle your enthusiasm for cycling. If, however, you seek company for your rides, or further information, you will have no trouble locating groups and publications ready to meet your needs. There are so many such organizations, in fact, that we cannot possibly list them all or give information that will stay current. We can get you started.

ORGANIZATIONS

These leading organizations provide a wealth of information for the novice bicyclist. You'll be able to choose one that has the right orientation for your interests.

ADVENTURE CYCLING ASSOCIATION
PO Box 8308
Missoula, MT 59807
406-721-1776
Formerly known as Bikecentennial, the non-profit Association acts both as a tour organizer and a clearinghouse of cycling information. An excellent source of maps and information for self-guided tours and a mail-order source of many of the books listed below. Also publishes The Cyclists' Yellow Pages, *an invaluable resource for maps, regional clubs, tour organizers, and much more—a virtual bible of the sport. Annual individual membership is $25, for which a copy of* The Yellow Pages *and other materials and benefits are offered.*

BICYCLE FEDERATION OF AMERICA
1506 21st Street NW, Suite 200
Washington, DC 20036
202-463-6622
The Federation is a non-profit organization promoting bike use throughout the U.S.A. Primary source of information and statistics on U.S. bike use. Publishes a monthly newsletter.

HOSTELING INTERNATIONAL-AMERICAN YOUTH HOSTELS
733 15th Street, #840
Washington, DC 20005
202-783-6161
Within the U.S., the organization operates 200 hostels across the country, and also acts as a group-tour organizer.

INTERNATIONAL HUMAN-POWERED VEHICLE ASSOCIATION
PO Box 51255
Indianapolis, IN 46251
317-876-9478
The Association promotes the innovation of human-powered vehicles for land, air, and water. Sponsors an annual speed championship for human-powered vehicles.

INTERNATIONAL MOUNTAIN BICYCLING ASSOCIATION
PO Box 412043
Los Angeles, CA 90041-9043
818-792-8830
IMBA is dedicated to promoting "soft" — socially and environmentally responsible — mountain biking.

LEAGUE OF AMERICAN BICYCLISTS
190 West Ostend Street,
Suite 120
Baltimore, MD 21230
410-539-3399
The League serves primarily non-racing cyclists: commuters, tourers, recreational riders, etc.; promotes government support of cycling as a transportation alternative; and publishes a magazine eight times a year.

NATIONAL BICYCLE DEALERS ASSOCIATION
2240 University Drive, #130
Newport Beach, CA 92660
714-722-6909
If you're looking for a good bike shop in your area, the NBDA may be a useful source of information.

NATIONAL OFF-ROAD BICYCLING ASSOCIATION
1750 E. Boulder
Colorado Springs, CO 80909
719-578-4717
NORBA is the national governing body of mountain-bike racing in the U.S.

RAILS-TO-TRAILS CONSERVANCY
1400 16th Street NW, Suite 300
Washington, DC 20036
202-797-5400
The non-profit Conservancy is working to convert thousands of miles of abandoned railroad tracks in the U.S. to bike trails.

SURFACE TRANSPORTATION POLICY PROJECT
1400 16th Street N.W.
Suite 300
Washington, D.C. 20036
202-939-3470
Works to improve conditions for cyclists and pedestrians.

UNITED STATES BICYCLING HALL OF FAME
166 West Main Street
Somerville, NJ 08876
800-BICYCLE
The Hall is dedicated to preserving the history of U.S. bicycling.

UNITED STATES CYCLING ASSOCIATION
1 Olympic Plaza
Colorado Springs, CO 80909
719-578-4581
The USCA is the governing body for road and track racing in the U.S. Publishes a monthly magazine.

WOMEN'S CYCLING COALITION
PO Box 7313
Loveland, CO 80537
303-669-5940
Non-profit organization promoting better women's cycling on both the recreational and racing levels.

TOUR ORGANIZERS

There are dozens of bike-tour organizers in the U.S. Those included here are possibly the best-known and most reputable. A more comprehensive list of tour organizers can be found in *The Cyclists' Yellow Pages* (see page 181).

ADVENTURE CYCLING ASSOCIATION
see listing on page 181

BACKROADS
1516 5th Street
Berkeley, CA 94710
800-462-2848.
With close to 100 trips a year in the U.S. and around the world, Backroads is the biggest bike-tour organizer in the country.

BREAKING AWAY BICYCLE TOURS
1142 Manhattan
Manhattan Beach, CA 90266
310-545-5118.
Breaking Away specializes in tours in conjunction with the Tour de France, the world's premier cycling event. Ride some of the race route, check out some of the race action, feast on French food.

BUTTERFIELD & ROBINSON
70 Bond Street
Toronto, ON M5B 1X3
800-678-1147
B & R likes going in style, mixing bike touring with plenty of fancy food and posh lodging.

ELK RIVER TOURING CENTER
Highway 219
Slatyfork, WV 26291
304-572-3771.
Elk River is indeed the center of mountain biking in West Virginia, the hot spot of East Coast off-road riding.

RIM TOURS
94 West 1st North
Moab, UT 84532
800-626-7335.
The hot spot of Western off-road riding is Moab. Rim Tours, based in Moab's renowned Rim Cyclery, is the granddaddy of mountain-bike tour organizers.

ROADS LESS TRAVELED
PO Box 8187
Longmont, CO 80501
800-488-8483.
RLT does a good job of leading road trips as well as off-road adventures, if you've got a taste for both.

TIMBERLINE BICYCLE TOURS
7975 E. Harvard #J
Denver, CO 80231
303-759-3804
On a typical Timberline tour, the daily riding (on the road) is usually robust, with the twin rewards of fine food and cushy lodging at day's end.

VERMONT BICYCLE TOURING
Box 711
Bristol, VT 05443
802-453-4811
VBT is one of the originals and one of the best. But note that the company offers tours all over the U.S., as well as in Europe and New Zealand.

WESTERN SPIRIT CYCLING
32 South 100 West
Moab, UT 84532
801-259-8732
Fax: 801-259-2736
Tours of the "slick rock" area of Utah—one of the Meccas of mountain bicycling in North America—and beyond.

MAGAZINES

The established bicycling magazines can both thrill and lend assurance to those new to the sport. They are chock full of techniques, recommendations, and usually ample back sections with advertisements for outfitters, organizations and trips.

BICYCLE GUIDE
6420 Wilshire Boulevard
Los Angeles, CA 90048
213-782-2000
Contains regular features on mountain biking and equipment.

BICYCLING
Rodale Press
33 Minor Street
Emmaus, PA 18098
610-967-8181.
This is the nation's leading magazine on cycling, covering all aspects of the sport, but with a principal focus on road riding and touring.

BIKE
PO Box 1028
Dana Point, CA 92629
714-496-5922.
As mountain biking grows, so do the number of magazines devoted to it. Bike *is one of the newest and one of the best.*

BMX PLUS!
PO Box 957
Valencia, CA 91380-9057
For BMX and bicycle freestylers.

CROSSWORDS
PO Box 3207
Walnut Creek, CA 94598
510-975-4522
Hybrid bike news.

CYCLING SCIENCE
Pike Creek Press Inc.
PO Box 1497
Los Altos, CA 94023-1497
415-949-2072
The scientific side of bicycling is illuminated by engineers, inventors and sports scientists.

IBF NEWS
4887 Columbia Drive So.
Seattle, WA 98108-1919
Published by the non-profit International Bicycle Fund, promoting sustainable transport.

KOKOPELLI NOTES
A Journal of Self-Propelled Transportation
PO Box 8186
Asheville, NC 28814
704-683-4844
A "green" magazine about transportation choices.

MOUNTAIN AND CITY BIKING
7950 Deering Ave
Canoga Park, CA 91304
818-887-0550
FAX 818-883-3019
For both on- and off-road enthusiasts.

MOUNTAIN BIKE
Rodale Press
33 Minor Street
Emmaus, PA 18098
610-967-8181.
An off-road off-shoot of Bicycling, *this is the circulation leader in the mountain-bike-mag field.*

MOUNTAIN BIKE ACTION
PO Box 957
Valencia, CA 91380-9057
For mountain bikers.

OUTSIDE
Outside Plaza
400 Market Street
Santa Fe, NM 87501
505-989-7100.
Outside *includes, among its broad coverage of outdoor sports and environmental issues, features, travel reports, and equipment reviews related to cycling.*

PEDAL MAGAZINE
2 Pardee Suite 204
Toronto, Ontario
M6K 3H5 Canada
416-530-1350
FAX: 416-530-4155
Canada's national cycling magazine.

PETERSEN'S BICYCLE GUIDE
6420 Wilshire Boulevard
Los Angeles, CA 90048-5515
213-782-2349
General interest magazine.

RECUMBENT CYCLIST NEWS
PO Box 58755
Renton, WA 98058-1755

TRIATHLETE
744 Roble Rd, #190
Allentown, PA 18103-9110
215-266-6893
800-441-1666
A monthly magazine for triathletes.

VELO-NEWS
Inside Communications
1830 N. 55th Street
Boulder, CO 80301
303-440-0601.
This is the racer's journal, covering the national and international scene for both road racing and mountain biking.

CD-ROMS

Try these newest of the multimedia products available for your home use.

Bicycling's Index on Disk, product reviews, training tips, fitness advice and dealer locator, $12.95, to order call 800-551-6634 or download the Index from Bicycling Magazine Online (AOL) software library.

Mountain Biking, CD Rom Skill Services for Outdoor Sports, for Windows and Mac from Media Mosaic, $59.95, from Backcountry Bookstore, 206-290-7652.

THE INTERNET

It comes as no surprise that surfing the Internet for bicycle-related news is a profitable activity! Remember that things change swiftly on the Net, so all information that we provide below can only be guaranteed at the time of publication. To get started, try:

http://www.cs.purdue.edu/homes/dole/bike.html
From the WWW Bicycle Home Page you can access gopher sites, membership applications, the online version of *Cycling Plus* (a British publication), all sorts of racing news, and an ftp directory.

People Power Update is an electronic newsletter of the bicycle advocacy group People Power. Address of contact Ron Goodman is *goodman@cats.uscs.edu* and the group is accessible at *gopher.well.sf.ca.us.* A discussion group "all about human-powered cycling" can be joined by sending a message to *listserv@bitnic.edcom.edu,* with the message subscribe bicycle first-name last-name. Check out the newsgroup *rec.bicycles* for information on buying, selling and reviewing cycling equipment, a discussion of racing rules and results, and lots more.

For those of you considering subscribing to a commercial on-line provider, *America Online* (AOL) has two outdoor services. Belonging to AOL is a good way to access other groups. To subscribe, call 800-827-6364, Ext. 10380. The software will be provided to you free.

TRAILSIDE®: MAKE YOUR OWN ADVENTURE

Trailside's service can be accessed via keyword "Trailside." The service has up-to-date information from the television series program guides and station listings as well as an active bulletin board, Campfire Chats, Trailside Outfitter, Maps and Snaps, News and Reviews, and complete gear lists from ongoing Trailside adventures. By subscribing to America Online you can access *Bicycling Magazine* as well.

OUTDOOR ADVENTURE ONLINE

This travel and recreation service lists outfitters, organizations, and providers of lodging. It also has an active message board for travelers.

BOOKS

If you like to read or feel better easing slowly into this new venture, here are some suggestions. There are excellent guides for repairs and countless suggestions for making your outings more comfortable and more fun.

BASICS AND MAINTENANCE

Anybody's Bike Book, Tom Cuthbertson. 1990. Paper. $9.95 Ten Speed Press. Two decades after its initial publication, this continues on as a classic maintenance manual for cyclists with little mechanical inclination.

The Basic Essentials of Mountain Biking, Michael Strassman. 1989. $5.99. ICS.

Bicyclng Magazine's Cycling for Women, The Editors of *Bicycling.* 1989. $4.95. Rodale Press. A publication addressing the particular needs of women cyclists.

Bicycling Magazine's Six Hundred Tips for Better Bicycling, The Editors of *Bicycling.* 1991. $6.95. Rodale Press. The tips cover everything from nutrition to technique and come from respected authorities in the world of cycling.

Bicycling Science, Frank R. Whitt & David G. Wilson. 1982. $14.50 (Hardcover is out of print). MIT Press. The information can be cumbersomely scientific and some of the data is dated, but this research compendium is still an enlightening survey of the physics and mechanics of cycling.

Bicycling Magazine's Complete Guide to Bicycle Maintenance & Repair, the Editors. 1994. $24.95/$16.95. Rodale Press: Emmaus, PA). This is a complete, nuts-and-bolts guide, including up-to-date instruction for mountain-bike repair.

Bike Touring: The Sierra Club Guide to Outings on Wheels, Raymond Bridge. 1979. $10.95. Sierra Club.

Cycling Health & Physiology: Using Sports Science to Improve Your Riding & Racing, Edmund R. Burke. 1992. $16.95. Vitesse Press. The book is geared for racers and dedicated riders, but anyone interested in developing a scientific training program should benefit from it.

Essential Touring Cyclist: a Complete Course for the Bicycle Traveler, Richard A. Lovett. 1994. $15.95. McGraw-Hill.

Greg LeMond's Complete Book of Bicycling, Greg LeMond and Kent Gordis. 1990. $11.00. Perigee Books. Lemond made his mark as three-time winner of the Tour de France. The book covers all aspects of road riding, from buying a bike to basic maintenance, with a strong emphasis on race training, technique, and tactics.

Mountain Bike! A Manual of Beginning to Advanced Technique, William Nealy. 1992. $12.95. Menasha Ridge Press. The flip, cartoon-style approach to basic mountain-bike technique may be visually jarring, but the information is sound and useful.

A Mountain Bike Way of Knowledge, William Nealy. 1989. $6.95. Menasha Ridge.
Mountain Bikes: Maintenance &

Repair, John Stevenson. 1994. $22.50. Bicycle Books. Yes—mountain bikes are a breed of their own, requiring their own maintenance and repair procedures. The illustrations go a long way toward clarifying those procedures.

Richards' Ultimate Bicycle Book, Richard Ballentine and Richard Grant. 1992. $29.95. Dorling Kindersley. If riding itself isn't enough to get you psyched about cycling, a handsome book such as this one ought to convince you.

Sloane's New Bicycle Maintenance Manual, Eugene A. Sloane. 1991. $14.95. Simon & Schuster. This book is not new at all; it has been around for many years and has been revised regularly. One of the best, most detailed maintenance manuals you can find.

A Woman's Guide to Cycling. (Adventure Cycling Association: Missoula, MT). Friendly tips for the female rider.

WHERE-TO GUIDES

Just a sampling of what's available in the way of detailed guides to bicycle routes.

The Best Bike Rides in New England, Paul Thomas. 1993. $12.95. Globe Pequot Press. More than 40 suggested trips.

Best Bike Rides in the Pacific Northwest, Todd Litman & Suzanne Kort. 1992. $12.95. Globe Pequot Press. 50 single-day bicycle tours in three states, plus British Columbia.

Bicycling the Atlantic Coast: A Complete Route Guide, Florida to Maine, Donna Aitkenhead. 1993. $14.95. Mountaineers Books. A guide to bicycling 2700 miles through 15 states.

Bicycling the Blue Ridge: A Guide to the Skyline Drive and the Blue Ridge Parkway, Elizabeth & Charlie Skinner. 1990. $10.95. Menasha Ridge Press. This is a "complete" book: for camping, sightseeing, whatever you may need while you bike.

Bicycling the Pacific Coast: a Complete Route Guide, Canada to Mexico, Tom Kirkendall and Vicky Spring. 1990. $12.95. Mountaineers Books. Details of 1,947 miles of riding.

Cycling the U.S. Parks: Fifty Scenic Bicycle Tours in America's National Parks, Jim Clark. 1993. $12.95. Bicycle Books. Family bicycling through 30 spectacular national parks.

500 Great Rail-Trails, Rails-to-Trails Conservancy (Washington, DC). 6,000 miles of trails in 44 states.

The Pacific Crest Bicycle Trail, Paul Bil. 1991. $13.95. Bittersweet Publishing. A guide to this 2,500 mile route.

Touring New England by Bicycle, Peter Powers. 1991. $10.95. Twenty trips in three states, with unique computer-generated maps.

25 Bicycle Tours on Delmarva, John Wennersten. 1988. $10.00. Countryman Press. Biking in Delaware, Maryland and Virginia.

VIDEOS

Our own Trailside® series of videos which aired on Public Television are perhaps the best inspiration we can offer to the novice cyclist. Included are tips and techniques from experts and professionals, led in each video by John Viehman, executive editor of *Backpacker* magazine and Trailside's host and series editor. The following videos and others in the Trailside® series may be purchased by calling 800-TRAILSIDE (800-872-4574). Catalog available.

Trailside's Mountain Biking in Utah. Host John Viehman with experts teach the basics of gear, equipment and technique riding the gnarly switchbacks of Moab. Includes behind-the-scenes footage and hints and tips. 45 minutes, $19.98.

Trailside's Bike Touring Through the California Redwoods. Pedal the rugged California coast while learning the ins and outs of bike touring, from climbing steep grades to banking hairpin curves among the old-growth giants in Humboldt Redwoods State Park. Includes behind-the-scenes footage and hints and tips. 45 minutes, $19.98.

Trailside's Family Mountain Biking in South Dakota. Off-road family adventure in the rugged Black Hills of South Dakota; pedal through scenic meadows, watch free-roaming buffalo and learn rough terrain biking skills. Includes behind-the-scenes footage and hints and tips. 45 minutes, $19.98.

A SAMPLING OF OTHER VIDEOS

Complete Bicycle Maintenance & Overhaul, Video University Productions, 53 minutes, $19.95, Backcountry Bookstore, 206-290-7652.

Fundamentals of Bicycle Maintenance. REI mechanics explain the basics for mountain and road bikes. 55 minutes, $34, Elliott Bay Film Company, 206-784-4666 or Backcountry Bookstore, 206-290-7652.

Fundamentals of Bicycle Touring. 60 minutes, $29.95, Elliott Bay Film Company, 206-784-4666 or Backcountry Bookstore, 206-290-7652.

Great Mountain Biking Video. An introduction to the sport. 50 minutes, $19.95, New & Unique Videos, 619-282-6126.

John Howard's Lessons in Cycling. An experienced racing coach shares his knowledge. 60 minues, $29.95, New & Unique Videos, 619-282-6126.

L. L. Bean Guide to Bicycle Touring. How to have fun touring, from selecting a bike to roadside repairs; shot in Acadia National Park. 80 minutes, $29.95. L. L. Bean, 800-221-4221

Ultimate Mountain Biking. For advanced mountain bikers and racers. 60 minues, $24.95, New & Unique Videos, 619-282-6126.

MAIL-ORDER SOURCES OF BOOKS & VIDEOS

Adventurous Traveler Bookstore. PO Box 577 Hinesburg, VT 05461; 800-282-3963 or 802-482-3330. FAX 800-282-3963, 802-482-3546. E-mail: *books@atbook.com*; on the World Wide Web — *http://www.gorp.com/atbook.htm* — search their full selection of 3,000 titles by keyword. Largest supplier of worldwide adventure travel books & maps.

ALL ADVENTURE TRAVEL
800-537-4025.

BACKCOUNTRY BOOKSTORE
PO Box 6235
Lynnwood, WA 90836-0235
206-290-7652
Books and videos on all outdoor activities, as well as knowledgeable staff.

L. L. BEAN
Casco Street
Freeport, ME 04032
800-727-6689
Retail store in Freeport, outlets and catalog sales. Books, videos, and audio tapes.

VIDEO ACTION SPORTS
200 Suburban Road, Suite E
San Luis Obispo, CA 93401
800-727-6689 or 805-543-4812.

MAIL-ORDER SOURCES OF ACCESSORIES

Ordering clothing and equipment from catalogs is standard procedure for serious cyclists, especially those who might not live within shouting distance of a well-stocked bike shop. Most mail-order companies offer next-day delivery service. It's a good idea is to get more than one catalog in order to compare prices. Prices are typically equal to or lower than those in well-stocked shops.

BIKE NASHBAR
4111 Simon Road
Youngstown, OH 44512
800-NASHBAR

BRANFORD BIKE
1074 Main Street
Dept B-9
Branford, CT 06405
800-272-6367
fax: 203-483-0703

COLORADO CYCLIST, INC.
3970 E. Bijou Street
Colorado Springs, CO 80909
800-688-8600

EXCEL SPORTS BOULDER
2045 32nd Street
Boulder, CO 80301
800-627-6664
fax: 303-444-7043

L. L. BEAN
Casco Street
Freeport, ME 04032
800-221-4221

PERFORMANCE BICYCLE
PO Box 2741
Chapel Hill, NC 27514
800-727-2453

REI
Dept. N5001
Sumner, WA 98352-0001
800-426-4840, ext. N5001

WOMYN'S WHEEL
PO Box 2820
Orleans, MA 02653-0015
800-795-7433

BIKE MANUFACTURERS

Here is a list of the major bicycle manufacturers. Try calling them for a catalog.

AEGIS
Champlain Street
PO Box 69
Van Buren, ME 04785
207-868-3909; 800-792-3447

ALPINESTARS
3801 Del Amo #401
Torrance, CA 90503
310-542-5996; 800-727-8277

AMERICAN FLYER, INC.,
28 Fox Lane, Carriage House
Mount Kisco, NY 10549
914-234-3860

BIANCHI
21371 Cabot Boulevard
Hayward, CA 94545
510-264-1001; 800-431-0006

BOULDER BICYCLES
Box 1400
Lyons, CO 80540
303-532-0133
Custom mountain bikes.

CANNONDALE
9 Brookside Pl.
Georgetown, CT 06829-0122
800-Bike-USA; 203-544-9800
All types of bikes, all aluminum frames, mid-price and up.

DEAN
2525 Arapahoe, E4
Boulder, CO 80302
303-530-3091; 800-545-2535

DIAMOND BACK (WSI)
4030 Via Pescador
Camarillo, CA 93012
805-484-4450; 800-776-7641
Reasonably priced, highly rated mountain bikes.

FISHER
801 W. Madison
Waterloo, WI 53594
800-688-4324; 800-783-4744

FUJI
118 Bauer Drive
Oakland, NJ 07436
201-337-1700; 800-631-8474

GIANT BICYCLE, INC.
475 Apra Street, Rancho Dominguez, CA 90220
310-609-3340; 800-874-4268
Mountain bikes and road bikes, budget and moderately priced.

GT BICYCLES, INC.
3100 W. Segerstrom Avenue
Santa Ana, CA 92704
714-841—7791; 800-RID-EAGT
Reasonably priced, highly rated mountain bikes.

IBIS
PO Box 275
Sebastopol, CA 95473
707-829-5615

JAMIS
distributed by
G. Joannou Cycle
151 Ludlow Avenue
Northvale, NJ 07647
201-768-9101; 800-222-0570
Reasonably-priced, high-quality road and mountain bikes.

KLEIN BICYCLE CORP.
118 Klein Road
Chehalis, WA 98532
206-262-3305
Custom component mountain bikes.

KONA MOUNTAIN BIKES
1122 Fir Avenue
Blaine, WA 98230
206-332-5384

LITESPEED TITANIUM
Box 22666
Chattanooga, TN 37422
615-238-5530

MARIN MOUNTAIN BIKES
16 Mary Street
San Rafael, CA 94901
415-485-5100; 800-222-7557
High-end mountain bikes.

MONGOOSE
23879 Madion Street
Torrance, CA 90505
310-539-8860

MOTIV SPORTS INC.
14211 Yorba Street
Tustin, CA 92680
714-731-6011

NISHIKI
22710 72nd Avenue South, Kent, WA 98032
206-395-1100

NORCO PRODUCTS USA
18201 Olympic Avenue South
Tukwila, WA 98188
206-251-9370; 800-521-9088

NORCO PRODUCTS LTD.
7950 Enterprise Street,
Burnaby, BC, Canada V5A 1V7
604-420-6616

NOVARA (REI)
6750 South 228th Street
Kent, WA 98032
206-395-3780.

PARKPRE BICYCLES
5245 Kazuko Ct.
Moorpark, CA 93021
805-529-5865; 800-727-5773
Budget suspension mountain bikes.

PEUGEOT (PROCYCLE)
PO Box 810
Hackensack, NJ 07602
201-489-3533; 800-543-4142

PEUGEOT (PROCYCLE)
9095 25th East Avenue Parc Ind, Street Georges
PQ, Canada, G6A 1A1
418-228-8934

RALEIGH USA BICYCLE
22710 72nd Avenue South
Kent, WA 98032
206-395-1100; 800-222-5527
Full-range, all types road and mountain bikes.

RESEARCH DYNAMICS
PO Box 3290
Hailey, ID 83333
208-788-3100, 800-782-0809

RITCHEY USA
1326 Hancock St
Redwood City, CA 94020
415-368-4018

ROCKY MOUNTAIN BICYCLES
1322 Cliveden Avenue
Delta, BC, Canada V6V 1Z1
604-270-2710; 800-663-2512
High-end mountain bikes.

ROSS BICYCLES
51 Executive Boulevard
Farmingdale, NY 11735
516-249-6000; 800-338-7677

SCHWINN BICYCLE COMPANY
1690 38th Street
Boulder, CO 80301
303-939-0100
Full line of road and mountain bikes.

SCOTT USA
Box 2030
Sun Valley, ID 83353
208-622-1000; 800-292-5874

SEROTTA COMPETITION BICYCLES
PO Box 1439
South Glen Falls, NY 12803
518-747-8620; 800-338-0998
High-end racing and touring bikes.

SPECIALIZED
15130 Concord Circle
Morgan Hill, CA 95037
408-779-6229; 800-245-3462
Moderately priced road and mountain bikes.

TERRY PRECISION BICYCLES
1704 Wayneport Road
Macedon, NY 14502
315-986-2103; 800-289-8379
Specializes in bikes built for women, accessories too.

TIMBERLIN (WISCONSIN CYCLE SUPPLY CO.)
2932 Brens Parkway
Sheboygan, WI 53091
414-458-9171; 800-558-7787

TREK BICYCLE CORPORATION
801 W. Madison Street
Waterloo, WI 53594
414-478-2191; 800-879-8735

UNIVEGA (LAWEE, INC.)
3030 Walnut Avenue
Long Beach, CA 90807
310-426-0474; 800-829-3040

PHOTO CREDITS

BOB ALLEN: 50 (bottom, 2nd from left), 52, 59, 78, 85, 86, 94, 101, 108 (all), 109 (top), 134, 154 (top), 165

DOUG BERRY: 93

DUGALD BREMNER: 46, 67, 75, 97, 102 (all), 105, 168

SKIP BROWN: 6, 18, 20, 91, 120, 122, 128, 170, 179

DENNIS COELLO: 13, 14, 16, 21, 31, 50 (top), 53, 57, 60 (right), 79, 81, 87, 90, 92, 113, 118, 121, 125, 129, 131, 140, 141, 147, 149, 150, 153, 154 (bottom), 155 (all), 167, 173

ERIC EVANS: 63, 133

MALCOLM FEARON/SINGLETRACK: 136

BOB FIRTH: 17, 50 (bottom, 3rd, 4th, 5th from left), 62, 82, 83, 88,

CARL GOODING: 11, 23, 24, 25, 26, 28, 29, 32, 33, 36, 37, 39, 40 (both), 41 (both), 44, 45 (both), 49, 50 (bottom, 1st from left), 51 (all), 55 (all), 60 (left), 61, 64 (both), 68 (all), 69 (all), 72 (both), 74 (both), 89 (both), 117, 126, 135, 148, 151, 157, 163 (both), 164, 169, 172 (top)

JOHN GOODMAN: 47

MARK JOHNSON: 27, 175, 176

JOHN KELLY: 43, 103, 107 (both), 109 (bottom), 110, 111 (all), 115, 161, 172 (bottom)

BECKY LUIGART-STAYNER: 146

SCOTT MERCER: 65

GLENN MOODY: 127

TOM MORAN/SINGLETRACK: 77, 98, 104, 112, 137, 138

NEAL PALUMBO/SINGLETRACK: 132

DOUG PLUMMER: 174

MICHAEL SHAW: 156, 160, 162 (all)

GRAHAM WATSON: 15

TERRY WILD: 119, 177

GORDON WILTSIE: 22

INDEX

T

U

V

W

Y